DAY TRADING STRATEGIES

(BOOK 2)

THE COMPLETE GUIDE WITH ALL THE ADVANCED
TACTICS FOR STOCK AND OPTIONS TRADING
STRATEGIES. FIND HERE THE TOOLS YOU WILL NEED TO
INVEST IN THE FOREX MARKET.

ANDREW ELDER

Table of Contents

Introduction

I t is essential that you understand and apply all these three elements in day trading. While some strategies only require technical indicators (like VWAP and Moving Average), it will help you a lot if you understand price action and chart patterns, so you can be a profitable day trader.

This knowledge, especially about price action comes only with regular practice. As a day trader, you must not care about the company and its revenue. You should not be distracted about the mission or vision of the company or how much money they make. Your focus must only be on the chart patterns, technical indicators, and price action.

Successful day traders also don't mix technical analysis with fundamental analysis. Day traders usually focus more on technical analysis.

The catalyst is the reason why a particular stock is running. If you have a stock that is running up to 70%, you need to determine the catalyst behind this change, and never stop until you figure that one out.

So, it's a tech company that just got patent approval or a pharmaceutical company that passed through important clinical trials. These are catalysts that can help you understand what is really going on.

Beyond this, don't bother yourself squinting over revenue papers or listening in conference calls. You should not care about these things unless you are a long-term investor.

Day traders trade fast. There are times that you may find yourself trading in time periods as short as 10 to 30 seconds, and can make thousands of dollars. If the market is moving fast, you need to make certain that you are in the right position to take advantage of the profits, and minimize your exposure to risk.

There are millions of day traders out there with different strategies. Each trader requires its own strategy and edge. You must find your spot in the market whenever you feel comfortable.

You must focus on day trading strategies because these really work for day trading. The following strategies have been proven effective in day trading. These strategies are quite basic in theory, but they can be challenging to master and requires a lot of practice.

Also remember that in the market today, more than 60% of the volume is dominated by algorithmic trading. So you are really competing against computers. There's a big chance that you will lose against an algorithm. You may get lucky a couple of times, but supercomputers will definitely win the game.

Trading stocks against computers means that the majority of the changes in stocks that you see are basically the result of computers moving shares around. On one hand, it also means that there are certain stocks every day that will be traded on such heavy retail volume.

Every day, you have to focus on trading these specific stocks or the Apex Predators - the stocks that are usually gapping down or up on revenue.

You should hunt for stocks that have considerable interest among day traders and considerable retail volume. These are the stocks that you can buy, and together, the retail traders can still win the game against algorithmic traders.

One principle in day trading that you may find useful is that you must only choose the setups that you want to master. Using basic trading methods that are composed of minimal setups are effective in reducing the stress and confusion, and will allow you to focus more on the psychological effect of trading. This will separate the losers from the winners.

Managing Your Day Trades

It is always intriguing when two day traders choose the same stock - the one short and the other long.

More often than not, both traders become profitable, proving that trader management and experience are more important than the stock and the strategy used by the trader.

Remember, your trade size will depend on the price of the stock and on your account and risk management. Beginners in day trading are recommended to limit the size of their shares below 1000.

For example, you can buy 800 shares, then sell half in the first target. You can bring your stop loss to break even. Then you can sell another 200 in the next target. You can keep the last 200 shares until you stop. You can always maintain some shares in case the price will keep on moving in your favor.

IMPORTANT: Professional day traders never risk their shares all at once.

They know how to scale into the trade, which means they buy shares at different points. They may start with 200 shares and then add to their position in different steps. For instance, for an 800-share trader, they could enter either 400/400 or 100/200/500 shares. When done properly, this is an excellent way to manage your trades and risks. But managing the position in the system can be overly difficult. Many newbies who may attempt to do this could end up over trading and may lose their money in slippage, commissions, and averaging down the losing stocks. Rare is the chance that you may scale into a trade. Still, there are times that you can do this, especially in high-volume trades.

However, you should take note that scaling into a trade increases your risk and beginners can use it improperly as a way to average down their losing positions. We have discussed this for the sake of information, and this is not recommended for beginners.

Even though they may appear the same, there's a big difference between averaging down a losing position and scaling into a trade. For newbies, averaging down a losing position can wipe out your account, especially with small accounts that are not strong enough for averaging down.

ABCD Pattern

The ABCD Pattern is the simplest pattern you can trade, and this is an ideal choice for amateur day traders. Even though this is pretty much basic and has been used by day traders for a long time, it still works quite effectively because many day traders are still using it.

This pattern has a self-fulfilling prophecy effect, so you just follow the trend.

The chart above shows an example of an ABCD pattern in the stock market. This one begins with a strong upwards move.

Buyers are quickly buying stocks as represented by point A, and making new highs in point B. In this trend, you may choose to enter the trade, but you must not be overly obsessed with the trade, because at point B, it can be quite extended and at its highest price.

Moreover, you can't ascertain the stop for this pattern. Take note that you should never enter a trade without identifying your stop. At point

B, traders who purchased the stock earlier begin gradually selling it for profit and the prices will also come down.

Still, you must not enter the trade because you are not certain where the bottom of this trend will be. But if you see that the price doesn't come down from a specific level such as point C, it means that the stock has discovered possible support.

Thus, you can plan your trade and set up the, stops and a point to take the profits.

For example, OPTT (Ocean Power Technologies Inc) announced in 2016 that they closed a new $50 million deal. This one is a good example of a fundamental catalyst. OPTT stocks surged from $7.70 (Point A) to $9.40 (B) at around 9 am. Day traders who were not aware of the news waited for point B and then an indication that the stock will not go lower than a specific price (C).

If you saw that C holds support and buyers are fighting back to allow the stock price to go any lower than the price at C, you will know that the price will be higher. Buyers jumped on massively.

Remember, the ABCD Pattern is a basic day trading strategy, and many retail traders are looking for it. Near point D, the volume immediately spiked, which means that the traders are now in the trade. When the stock made a new low, it was a clear exit signal.

Here are the specific steps you can follow to use the ABCD strategy:

1. Whenever you see that a stock is surging up from point A and about to reach a new high for the day (point B), then wait to see if the price makes support higher than A. You can mark this as point C, but don't jump right into it.

2. Monitor the stock during its consolidation phase, then choose your share size and plan your stop and exit.

3. If you see that the price is holding support at point C, then you can participate in the trade closer to the price point C to anticipate the move to point D or even higher.

4. Your stop could be at C. When the price goes lower than C, you can sell. Thus, it is crucial to buy the stock closer to C to reduce the loss. (Some day traders have a higher tolerance, so they wait a bit more near D to ensure that the ABCD pattern is complete. However, this is risky as it can reduce your profit).

5. When the price moves higher, you can sell half of your shares near point D, and bring your stop higher to your breakeven point.

6. Sell the rest of your shares as soon as you hit your target or you feel that the price is losing momentum, or that the sellers are getting control of the price action.

Bull Flag Momentum

Expert stock analysts consider the Bull Flag Momentum as a scalping strategy because the flags in the pattern don't usually last long. Plus, day traders should scalp the trade in order to get in quickly, make money, and then exit the market.

Below is an example of a Bull Flag pattern with one notable consolidation.

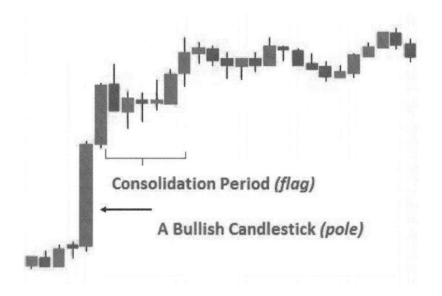

Consolidation Period *(flag)*

A Bullish Candlestick *(pole)*

This chart is called Bull Flag because it is like a flag on a pole. In this pattern, you have different large candles rising (pole) and you also have a sequence of small candles that move sideways (flag) or "consolidating" in day trading jargon.

When there is consolidation in the pattern, it signifies that traders who purchased the stocks at a lower price are now selling. While this is happening, the price doesn't significantly decrease because buyers are still participating in the trades, and sellers are not yet in control of the price. Many retail traders will miss buying the stock before the Bull Flag begins. Buying stocks when the price is increasing could be risky. This is known as "chasing the stock". Successful day traders usually aim to participate in the trade during quiet periods and take their profits during wild periods.

CHAPTER 1:

Know the Market

T he first thing to consider when getting started in day trading, is what market you want to use in order to trade. That may sound like an odd question to consider at this point, but depending on how much capital you have, choosing the right market is critical. The important thing to recognize with day trading is that day traders routinely have strings of losses. And we are not talking about amateurs here, experienced day traders will experience losses on a routine basis. Of course, you expect that over time you are going to make profits, but just like flipping a penny can result in 5 tails in a row, making many day trades can result in many losses before a big win hit. So, if you're trading a significant amount of your capital, a string of losses could leave you going broke very quickly. Thousands of dollars can be at stake in an individual trade. For these reasons, there are some rules and recommendations in place to help you avoid getting into super big trouble, but the rules may make day trading seem less appealing especially if you cannot come up with the required capital.

Things to consider before getting started

Day trading isn't a hobby or a game. It's a serious business, and just like any serious business day trading is going to require a serious commitment even before you get started.

- Day trading requires a serious time commitment. You are going to have to study the financial markets, keep up with financial news, and spend time at your computer pouring over financial data. Do you have the time to do all of these things? It's basically a full-time job. You're not going to be a day trader while working your 9-5 and expect to be successful. The day traders who are successful are 100% committed.

- Are you willing to practice before actually beginning day trading? Jumping in and risking tens of thousands of dollars without experience is a bad idea. We have listed links to practice software that lets you simulate stock market trading. Are you willing to spend several months honing your skills using practice methods before actually day trading with real money? You can even open "demo" accounts with many brokers. Consider working on this and practicing now, and then getting into real investing when you've honed your skills.

- Do you have adequate capital to get started? The U.S. government has a $25,000 minimum capital requirement to begin day trading. Do you have the money already? And is this actual money you can lose without getting into serious financial trouble?

Choose a broker

If you are already investing in stocks independently (that is outside an employer or a mutual fund) you may already have a broker that can also act as a broker for day trading purposes. Top brokers that retail investors can use include Ally Bank, TD Ameritrade, Trade Station, Interactive Brokers, ETrade, Charles Schwab, and many others.

Trading on the Stock Market

Of course, you can buy as few or as many shares of stock as you like, but experts advise that you need to have at least $25,000 in the capital that you can risk day trading in order to trade on the stock market. Making four trades in a week will qualify as being a day trader. If you plan to day trade four days per week, it's recommended that you have $30,000, in order to give yourself a bit of a buffer over the minimum. However, this value is quoted on the assumption that you're going to be trading actual shares of stock. It is recommended that your maximum risk on trade be limited to 1% of your total capital.

It's important to know your risk and position risk. Position risk is the number of shares times the risk. If you buy a stock at $20, and the stop-loss is $19, then your risk is $1. If you buy 500 shares, then your position risk is:

500 x ($20-$19) = $500

Stocks with higher volatility will require more risk than stocks with lower volatility. A day trader of stock can access leverage, typically at a rate of 4:1, allowing them to access more shares of stock than they could afford with their own capital.

A good way to get in on day trading on the stock market is --- you guessed it – by trading options. Buying an options contract only requires that you invest in the premium. Trading in options lets you leverage your money.

Futures Markets

You can day trade on futures markets with less capital. This can still let you get involved with stocks, however. For example, you can day trade the S&P 500 on the futures markets with a fraction of the capital required for day trading stocks. You can probably get started on this for between $1,000-$2,500. The daily range of futures can run from 10-40 points depending on volatility.

FOREX Markets

Forex markets are the lowest priced opportunity, with an entry level of capital of about $500. If you are interested in getting into day trading but lack capital, the FOREX markets can be an option to consider in order to get started with day trading. Even though FOREX markets have smaller required minimum accounts, the same rules apply. Traders should not risk more than 1% of their capital on a single trade. If you have a $2,000 account, then the most you'll want to risk on a trade is $20. While FOREX markets might appeal to you because of the smaller minimums, this is an entirely different world, with its own lingo and so forth. That isn't to say that getting some experience in the FOREX markets might be a good idea before risking massive amounts of capital day trading stocks. It very well might be an option to consider in order to use a real testing ground for day trading. This market will require you to study international trade and to spend time analyzing the global economy, rather than focus on individual companies. It's really a different animal, however, it can be complementary, and many traders do both.

Why Day Trade Options

Day trading stocks have a high barrier for entry because of capital requirements. You may or may not already be in a position to do it, but if you're not trading options provide a low barrier to entry alternative. There are several reasons to trade options rather than stocks. To begin with, trading options don't require hardly any money at all (in comparison) and it will allow you to gain experience looking at many of the same underlying fundamentals that day trading stocks require – since they are ultimately based on the same market.

- Options can be cheap. You can trade options at a much lower premium price as compared to the price required to buy stocks.
- Options offer huge upside potential. The percentage gains in options can be orders of magnitude larger than gains in stocks. So, you can invest a smaller amount of money, and reap larger gains on a percentage basis.

- You don't have to exercise the option to profit from it.

- Volatility makes trading stocks risky; it can make trading options profitable.

- The low price required to invest in options contracts means that you can often put together a diverse portfolio, even when making short term trades.

- It may be harder to get competitive spreads with options while day trading.

There are some downsides to day trading options. One important factor is that when day trading options, time value may limit short term changes in price. Options are also less liquid than the underlying stocks, so that can mean wider bid-ask spreads. Trading options will require you to get the same basic knowledge of day trading that we covered when discussing stocks. Ultimately, the value of the option is determined by the value of the underlying asset – the stock price.

Things to watch day trading options

Let's take a look at some indicators specific to options that you'll want to pay close attention to.

- Put/Call Ratio. If this is high, that means more traders are investing in puts for the underlying asset. In other words, the outlook is bearish because more traders are betting against the underlying or shorting it.

- Money Flow Index. This helps identify overbought and oversold assets. It tells you the flow of money that goes into the underlying asset or out of it over a specified period of time. Money flow takes into account both price and volume.

- Open Interest – this is the total number of outstanding options contracts that have not been settled.
- Relative strength and Bollinger bands.

Best Tools to Operate Day Trading

Day traders may have special needs to act fast and get information as quickly as possible in ways that normal stock investors don't require. One of the most important things a day trader needs is access to breaking news related to the markets.

CHAPTER 2:

How to Manage Risk in Day Trading:
Stop Loss and Take Profit

Step Risk Management

All organizations face unexpected risks, be it natural calamities or those caused by people. For instance, loss of finances or a member of an organization getting injured. These events can cost your organization to lose a lot of money which may in return, make the company eternally close. It is therefore important for a company to ensure that one puts strategies that would help in curbing such cases. With risk plan management in your company, you are prepared for a disaster. This is because it will help you to minimize the risk and also the cost you may incur. The risk plan will help you to set aside some amount of money so that it will protect your company in the future if stricken by disaster.

Risk management is a process of finding out the possible risk or disaster before it strikes. These give rooms for the owner of the company to organize his house by setting procedures of avoiding risk and reduce its ineffectiveness. An organization should have a realistic plan of the true level of risk evaluation. A risk management plan should be able to identify and able to deal with the risk. The plans don't need to be costly or should take more time for it to be implemented. Below is a risk management process.

Identifying Risk

You will identify risk by trying to look at it and finding what went wrong. There are many types of risks. They include the environmental risk and authoritarian risk as well as lawful risk and sell and buying risk. If the organization has a risk management tool, it becomes easy. This is because any information will be inserted into the system where it will be available when needed. The information will also be visible to all stakeholders. Being able to identify the risks that may be facing your company gives one a very positive experience.

One can also bring the whole team in the company to take part, which will be of help since they will give useful ideas on ways of managing risks. It will also be able to bring everyone on board and they will give varied experience based on what they have handled. As an employer, you will simply ask everyone to identify the risk they have experienced. The process will promote communication and it will also boost the employee's confidence. They will also be able to learn from each other's experiences. This is because the analysis will be from the management level of the company to the staff members of the company.

Employers can use mind maps that can be used to visualize the possible risk of the plan. They will be useful in inspiring the team members to think outside the box. After that, the management and the group's members will sit down and breakdown the structures to see clearly where risk might emerge. Once you have compiled all the possible issue creates a registered tool that will be used for following and observing all the risk in the plan. When you have all the data it will be easy to manage the upcoming coercion.

Analyzing Risk

What will be the impact of the risk in our organization? Could it make us lose everything we have worked for? Once you have the problem at hand, it becomes very easy to deal with it. In this step, teamwork is also encouraged. Because the team will analyze all the risks and see which one is urgent in dealing with. Prioritizing the risk gives you the idea of how to deal with issues as a whole. You will pinpoint where the team should focus more. They should give workable solutions to each risk. This will speed up the process of dealing with the risk. The determining factors will be time, financial loss and the impact of the risk on the company. If each risk is scrutinized, it will unveil the common topics in the plan and it will simplify the management procedure in the future. When implementing a risk solution is important to map the risk in different credentials, strategies measures, and business progression. It means that the business will have a framework of which it will calculate the risk and make you know the risk they impose.

Controlling and Handling Risk

What can be done to prevent the risk from taking place? If we are already in that mess, how are we going to salvage it? The moment the risk has been identified, it becomes easy to administer medication. You will table your medication plan and dispatch it. You will start with the risk with the highest priority. Assign duties to the team members so that they can help you in dealing with the problem. For mitigation to be effective, you will need help from the team resources. With time you will be having a database of the past plans. It will be easy to deal with others' risks because you will have the risk logs with you. You will not be practical rather than reacting to the advance for more treatment. There are four major groupings.

Transferring a risk means that the whole or part of the risk can be moved to a certain part, but some costs will be incurred. Avoiding a risk means that no activity will be carried out that will have risk. This may be the best way to deal with risks; for instance, not joining a business because you want to avoid losing an also it makes you avoid the possibility of making a profit. Regarding retaining a risk, there are two methods of retention: the self-insurance and captive insurance. Retention risk means the losses from the company or organization will be retained due to the decision from the business company. Controlling risk can be done by either avoiding the risks or by controlling the loss from the organization.

For risk management to be effective, it should ensure that all members of the organization are committed. All the policies and methods should be established. The staff should have clear roles and responsibilities and are very accountable. The teams should also have adequate resources and tools to be able to deal with the risk. If this is done, the benefits could be there will be saving of funds, point in time profits possessions populace and property. Having a safe and conducive environment for the workers, visitors, and also customers. There can also be a reduction in the legal liability and make an increase in the stability of the operations.

Trading Psychology

Trading psychology is referred to as a trader's mental state as well as their emotions which enable them to make sound decisions which in return will dictate their success as well as failure in the trading business. It represents the character and behavior of individuals which affects their actions when trading. For a businessman to succeed in the trading business, they need to ensure that they are good when it comes to trading psychology. This is because trading psychology is helpful in ensuring that a trader makes informed decisions for his company. Their mental, as well as emotional aspects, are helpful in ensuring that they make the right decisions.

Greed and fear, as well as regrets, are emotions that play a vital role in the trading business. In a trading business, greed can be important as well as destructive. This is because when one is greedy, they will always be driven by the desire to make more and more money. A trader should, therefore, utilize it in a good way in order to ensure that they benefit from it. They should learn the situations where they should use greed and when they should not.

Greed is described as an irresistible feeling which makes one want to be in possession of more things than they actually need. Greed is something that is very difficult to overcome. It requires one to have a lot of discipline in order for them to overcome it. Greed makes a trader want to make more money than they already have. Greed is said to have great results when utilized in the bull market. This is because the more a trader stays in the trading business, the more he or she gains experience. The experience enables them to be able to explore all the available opportunities, which helps them to create more wealth. Greed is only destructive when one invests, and then the stock market drops. They may find themselves making losses which are not so good for business.

A trader can, however, overcome greed by ensuring that they come up with a trading plan. The plan will normally be centered on balanced investment decisions. This will help a lot in ensuring that one is not guided by emotions when making business decisions. A trader can even set rules which they cannot go against when it comes to trading. They can also set a specific amount of money that they are ready to win and even to lose daily. They will only have that amount so once they exhaust it, they will just stop and wait to trade another day. This will help them in ensuring that they are disciplined when it comes to investing since they will invest an amount of money that they are ready to lose.

Fear is defined as something that one perceives as a threat to their income and also to their profits. Fear is also beneficial because it encourages the trader to hold back whenever they want to take any step in the trading process. It can also be destructive as well as useful, which will depend on when it is applied. A trader may feel the urge to invest in something, but because of fear of failing, they will stop. For example, whenever a trader receives any bad news about the stock market or even about the market in general, they tend to panic since they do not know whether they are going to make losses or not. There are those whose fear may lead them to liquidate their shares in the market while there are those who will just continue investing. By withholding their shares, it may save them when the prices in the stock market fail but they may lose opportunities to make more money because of the same fear. It is therefore important for a trader to ensure that they find ways of overcoming their fears, especially in situations that they feel like they could make losses. They should take calculated risks in order for them to ensure that they do not make losses after investing their shares in the market. The traders can also study the market which will help them to be able to identify areas that they can invest in without fear. The last emotion to take into consideration when trading is regret. Many businessmen have found themselves engaging themselves in the trading process because of regrets in the other businesses they have engaged in.

If not careful, they may find themselves regretting investing in the trade business in a hurry. The regrets will come in when they lose money after investing. It is therefore important to ensure that as a trader, you carry out thorough research before investing your money in any business.

CHAPTER 3:

Quantitative Risk and Qualitative Risk

When talking of risk, we can divide it into two broad groups: quantitative risk and qualitative. By nature, the quantitative risk is easier to measure and track because a lot of it is just numbers. The most basic is your hit rate and payout ratio.

To get a better idea of your risk, though, you should be tracking the following at a minimum. These numbers will also help clarify the profitability of a strategy, so when you back-test something, make sure to run these numbers as well.

Average Risk Percentage

This is the percentage of your account you are risking per trade. Now, you'll find a lot of sources online saying you should not risk anything over 2% of your account. Personally, I find 2% ridiculously high for beginners.

Think of it this way. If you risk 2% per trade, after taking ten losses in a row, you'll be 20% underwater! Imagine investing your money in something and losing 20%! You might think it's unlikely that ten losses in a row will occur, but this is ignoring the odds.

Based on your hit rate, your strategy will have certain odds of losing streaks based on their size. So the odds of a 10-trade losing streak for a 35% hit rate strategy, theoretically, are 91%. In other words, extremely damn likely.

Your objective should be to protect your capital at all costs. Therefore, risking 2% when you have a 91% chance of experiencing a 20% drawdown (more on this below) is doing the exact opposite. As a beginner, your risk per trade should not be more than 0.25% of your account. This way, if you lose ten in a row, which is very likely, you'll be down just 2.5%, which is easily retrieved.

Drawdown

A drawdown is just the size of the loss you take, so if you lose a trade and are risking 0.25% per trade, your drawdown is 0.25%. More relevant is the max drawdown, which is what most traders refer to when reviewing a strategy's effectiveness. The max drawdown is the difference between the highest and lowest points of your account's equity curve.

So if you lost 10 or 20 trades in a row, your account's equity graph is going to dip. The difference between the start of the dip and the trough or bottom is the total drawdown. The max drawdown is the biggest total drawdown the strategy experiences.

Drawdown size is a function of the hit rate and the per-trade risk. A strategy with a high hit rate can still experience significant drawdown if the per-trade risk is high.

As a reference, if you have a drawdown of over 10%, your account is 99% unlikely to recover. In the professional world, any fund that loses 10% is simply shut down since the managers are unlikely to recover the amount, and it's just more profitable to shut down and open a new fund. For professional traders who can be fund managers or prop shop traders, a monthly drawdown of 2% is the limit for the former and 4% for the latter.

Now, those numbers are for professionals, and as a beginner, you should stick to the 2% goal. In other words, you should structure your per-trade risk in a way that it is remotely possible for you to hit the 2% even with a very probable losing streak. This is how you take care of the downside and let the upside take care of itself.

As you can imagine, risking 0.25% per trade is unlikely to get you rich quick or provide enough income for you to quit your job and give everyone the middle finger. If you're disappointed or feel let down by this, I suggest you read the introduction again to understand what trading is really about. You'll save yourself a lot of time by trying to understand whether it really is for you or not.

Risk Limits

You should have daily, weekly, and monthly drawdown limits. The monthly limit should be around 2% to 3% of your account. The weekly can be set at around 1%. As for the daily, you should set it as a number of losses instead of a percentage. If you're paying attention, you'll see that it will take just four losses to trigger your weekly drawdown limit.

As a beginner, it is essential for you to take as much feedback as possible. This means placing as many trades as you can. Therefore, in order to trade correctly and not hit your risk limits, you need to reduce your per-trade risk to levels far below 0.25%. If you cannot operate in the market with such a low-risk level, you need to gather more capital and demo trade in the meantime.

Why even have risk limits? After all, if the numbers work, doesn't it make sense to keep trading no matter what? Shutting down trading for the week or month if you hit the limits will deprive you of opportunities to make the money back, right?

Well, theoretically, this is correct. However, practically speaking, there is no way you will be able to maintain your composure and simply execute once you've experienced a losing streak. Think of it this way: Olympic athletes who have dedicated their entire lives to training for a specific event also have bad days. These are people whose sole focus is on training and mental conditioning.

Even someone like Michael Jordan had bad games and days when he wasn't at his best. We're all human after all, and unless you can figure out a way to train an algorithm to trade in a discretionary manner, you will need to relax and release the stress of a loss from your mind. Life happens, and you need to account for it in your trading.

The risk limits point to an issue that you're perhaps not aware of but is manifesting itself somehow, causing you to trade poorly. If you're risking 0.1% of your account and you lose 1% in a week, that's ten trades you've lost at a minimum. This is how proper risk management saves you from yourself.

Recovery Period

The recovery period is the time it takes for your account to recover from its max drawdown and form a new equity high. A recovery period that is less than a drawdown period is obviously desirable. So if your account was underwater for two months, a recovery period of one month or three weeks is an excellent metric.

The recovery period measures how robust your strategy is. Every strategy experiences losing streaks. The true measure is not how many times it falls but how far it falls and how soon it can get back up.

Qualitative Risk

We're now leaving the realms of numbers and entering your mind and your habits. Obviously, this is a more difficult thing to measure, and a lot of it ties in with your mindset. Even if you're following a purely mechanical system of trading, you will still need to ensure your mind is prepared for trading in the best way possible.

Consistency and the degree to which you can repeat good habits are key to managing qualitative risk. While the numbers play an important part and your technical strategy takes care of your order entries, you still need to be of sound mind to execute them.

The following habits will calm your mind and prepare it for trading in an optimal way. It is essential for you to see how following these habits will not only make you money but also minimize your chances of losing it in the long run.

Exercise

Get moving and break out into a sweat. Do something to make sure you're exercising—be it walking, playing around with your dog, running, anything at all. Physical activity helps clear the cobwebs in your mind, and it helps you feel fresh and energized. You need to approach trading the same way a professional athlete approaches their game.

This means you must prepare your body for the trading session. While physically trading isn't demanding, you're going to be sitting and staring at a screen for quite some time. This puts stress on your body, and it is not good for your health. Exercise reduces this risk and keeps you fit and fresh.

Try to finish your workout a few hours before you trade. Trading right after a heavy workout isn't ideal for a number of reasons, which I hopefully don't need to go over.

Diet

While you can eat as unhealthy as you want and not have it affect your trading, this is more about just taking care of yourself so as to be as healthy as you can be. Remember, risk management is about managing your downside. If you're sick, you can't possibly trade, so preventing getting sick is far better than treating it.

While this isn't a diet book, make sure you are satiated and try not to eat anything heavy during the session. This causes you to get drowsy, and you might end up executing your strategy wrong.

Sleep

This one is non-negotiable. You cannot function on less than eight or how many ever appropriate hours of sleep you need. Some people think they can tough it out on just five or six hours, but this is simply idiotic. Your brain needs rest in order to function properly, and trading puts serious amounts of stress on your mind.

Therefore, you need to ensure you're well rested and make sleep a priority. Do whatever it takes to sleep well, and if you feel tired or lacking in energy during the trading day, walk away from the screen. The market will always be there, and you don't need to trade every single minute of it.

Lifestyle

If you routinely show up to your trading desk hung-over or, even worse, drunk on alcohol, you cannot possibly expect to make money. Too many people think trading is simply a matter of showing up and placing orders exactly as your technical system indicates, but this is simply not true.

Getting adequate rest and following proper discipline is what ensures success. You're increasing your risk massively by choosing to ignore these principles.

Mental Prep

The trading session is not the time and place for you to analyze anything. Your trade entries should be an automatic go/no-go decision. This boils down to how well you've practiced your strategy and have prepared yourself for the session.

This concludes our look at risk management. However, following and executing these principles will more than ensure your success.

CHAPTER 4:

Day Trading is Really Possibility to Business

Your Trading Success Plan

Failing to plan is planning to fail. How many of you have heard some version of this saying before? Trading is no exception when it comes to planning. You need to have a long-term plan of success that will serve as your reference guide, as well as a business plan.

Ultimately, trading is a business, and you need to keep meticulous records of performance like you would any business.

Trading Plans

You'll hear a lot of trading gurus tell you to make a plan. Well, what exactly is a trading plan, and why do you need one? To be honest, a trading plan by itself is not going to matter too much. However, when done right, it can help you focus and really nail down your vision when it comes to trading.

Perhaps a more appropriate term for this is to call it a trading business plan instead of just a trading plan. Much like how you need to record all key information (both financial and in terms of vision) in your business plan, your trading plan needs to do the same for your trading business. At a minimum, it needs to have the following information.

Instruments to Trade

What instruments will you be trading? List them all out here. You can even take this a step further and list out the individual stocks you will be trading. When starting out, it's best to pick a single instrument and trade just that.

This doesn't mean you go out and try to trade everything under the sun. You build a base with one, then two instruments, and then expand outward. Much like individuals, stocks have natures of their own in terms of liquidity and volatility. Some stocks have certain tendencies, depending on the time of the day.

You need to observe and learn all this in order to trade successfully, and doing so one by one is the way to go about it.

Markets and Timing

Which markets will you be trading? When will you trade them? So it is important for you to note down your session time and stick to it.

Which is the best session for beginners or busy people to trade? Well, there's no such thing as "best" to begin with. In terms of liquidity and best bang for your buck, the open is probably the best. The flip side to this is that the volatility can be pretty extreme. Things pick up toward the end of the day as well, so it's not as if the open is the only worthwhile time to trade.

The afternoon session is usually seen as something of a graveyard with a lot of traders stepping out for lunch. Don't just assume this is so. Observe the market and check its tendencies. While the more active stocks tend to slow down quite a bit, there are some instruments that provide easy pickings.

Capital and Risk per Trade

List out your trading capital and your risk per trade. If this reduced amount is too less for you to buy or sell any stock, then focus on getting more capital to start instead of increasing your risk per trade.

Risk Limits

What is your daily risk limit? Weekly, monthly, etc.? It is also a good idea to execute a gain-protection plan. What this means is that if you have a bunch of winners during the session (say two or more) or if you make a certain percentage of your account during the session (say anything about 0.5%), then you could decide to stop trading during that session if your gains dip below 0.25% or if you lose two more trades.

The idea is that you've made money during the session and you would like to hang on to it. This is to protect a string of winners or a huge gain. Once you've had a great day, it's perfectly fine to set a lower loss limit in order to protect some of it so that no matter what happens, you'll end the day up.

Technical System

Here's where you describe your technical trade entry system along with the exit strategy. I haven't covered a lot with regard to exit strategy because the exit or take-profit level depends on your hit rate. When designing your strategy, evaluate the most common payout it gives you. See if it makes money for you with its hit rate.

More advanced traders will include things like position sizing upon exit and such things. As a beginner, don't bother with partial exits. It'll only complicate your payout ratio calculations. Build and establish a good base, and you'll figure out whether you need partial exits or not.

A general rule of thumb is to aim for a payout ratio of 2. Anything below this requires a high hit rate, which very few systems provide. When exploring your system, remember that you can increase the hit rate by reducing the payout. You can play around with this to see if this makes the system more profitable for you.

Events

The markets have a bunch of external events that affect them, such as earnings announcements, dividends, splits, interest rate announcements, press conferences, and on and on. Generally speaking, you need to pay attention to the following events:

- earnings
- special events pertaining to the individual stock or political events like elections
- interest rate announcements
- nonfarm payrolls (NFP)

That's it. These events are always scheduled in advance, and as a beginner, stop trading an hour prior to the announcement and resume an hour after it has passed. The reason is that volatility jumps like crazy, and your stops will get triggered.

If you have any positions open that are close to profit, take a lower profit just before the announcement, as long as it doesn't affect your risk numbers too much. Similarly, if you have a trade that is in a loss and is near its stop-loss, you have to close the trade out just before the event.

If your trade is in the middle of the road or is even break even, ride the event out and hope for the best. Some stocks are better than others in this regard. Stay away from flashy companies run by Twitter-wielding CEOs who tend to send their products into space instead of building profits. You know who I'm talking about.

Aside from being annoying, you can bet there will be a number of algorithms and bots tracking every character such people type into Twitter, and all it takes for a flash tumble to occur in the stock is a typo or a rash tweet. Stick to boring names no one has heard of, and you'll be much better off, no matter how much you love or hate the company.

Review System

Every successful trader spends a lot of time reviewing their trades and actions over the week. Mention the time you will spend reviewing.

Practice

When will you practice your skills? What skills will you practice? Each strategy has a number of skills you need to execute, not to mention mental skills. Set aside time to practice each of these individually in order to perfect it.

Journals

As important as your trading plan is, the document that is of primary importance for your trading success is your trading journal. This will list all the trades you took over the past week and serve as a record for you to review. In addition to written records, you should also save screenshots of your trades on entry and exit.

Remember to also save screenshots of the market condition on the higher time frame on trade entry. Many times, on review, you will notice how you might have misjudged the higher time frame action. Below are the things your trading journal needs to record at a minimum:

- Date

- Instrument (the ticker or name of the stock)

- Entry price

- Stop-loss level

- Stop distance

- Position size

- Reasons for entry (describe in as much detail why this entry was in line with your strategy and what you saw)

- Reasons or exit

- Exit date

- P/L

- Mental state on entry

- Mental state on exit

You can either have this recorded on a spreadsheet or in a notebook; it doesn't matter where as long as you can review it easily. Save your screenshots in a numbered manner and in appropriate folders. In addition to this, you can also record your screen and yourself during the session and review your demeanor and market action at the time of entry to verify whether you were seeing things correctly.

Remember, the more information you record at the time, the more potential things there are for you to improve and learn.

Aside from the trading journal, you should also keep a mental journal. This is simply a record of what your mental state was during the session and if anything was bothering you at the time. It's up to you as to how much information you want to put in here, but you must aim to record whether you followed your preparation routines properly on that particular day.

Your prep routine can include physical exercise, meditation, visualization, affirmations, skill practice, and so on. It's up to you to decide what you want to include. Your aim should be to include things that are as repeatable as possible. Don't include too many things because you like the idea of it but will be stretched for time when it comes to implementing it.

The last journal you need to have is a review journal. You can incorporate this within your trade journal itself or as a separate document. When you're starting out, if it is logistically possible, I'd recommend reviewing your session after a 30-minute break once it ends. This way, the action is still fresh in your mind, and you're more relaxed.

Go through all your trades and review the screenshots. Review the video recording as well to confirm and check if what you saw was true. Record what you did incorrectly and, even more importantly, record what you did right. The review is not just about finding things to improve; it's also to celebrate things you did right.

Doing a review after each trading session will increase your rate of improvement as opposed to doing it weekly. Remember, even a session where you place no trades should be reviewed for mental state and whether you were tuned in or zoned out. Did you miss any opportunities? Leave no stone unturned.

Training

Trading is a unique endeavor in that we spend more time in the market (that is, game day) than in practice. Every other high-performance activity requires a minimum of double the amount of time to be spent in practice than in games. So how do you achieve this when it comes to trading?

CHAPTER 5:

Technical Analysis

Technical analysis is a method of looking at stock charts and data in order to spot price trends. It is a method primarily used by traders who are interested in short term profits, but it can be helpful for long-term investors as well. Long-term investors can use technical analysis to determine (estimate) the best entry points into their positions. Note that technical analysis certainly isn't required, and most long-term investors ignore short-term trends and use dollar cost averaging. Nonetheless, it's a good idea to become familiar with technical analysis in case you decide you want to use it in the future.

Technical vs. Fundamental Analysis

Technical analysis is different than fundamental analysis. They could be but aren't necessarily related. Fundamental analysis is focused on the underlying fundamentals of the company. These can include earnings, price to earnings ratio for the stock, and profit margins. The technical analysis ignores all of these things and is simply focused on the trades of the moment. It seeks to discover upcoming trends in buying behavior. So whether or not a company was profitable in the previous quarter – it doesn't necessarily matter. Of course, profitability can drive more stock purchases, and so drive up the price. But many things can drive the price up or down over the short term. Simple emotion can do it, and so traders that use technical analysis study the charts themselves and pay far less attention to external factors or fundamentals.

Trend Seeking

The first thing that technical analysis seeks to discover is the trend. Simply put, a trend is a prevailing price movement in one direction or the other. The time period isn't specific and will depend on the trader's needs and goals. For example, day traders are looking for a trend that might only last two hours. Swing traders may hope to ride a trend that lasts weeks or months. Position traders are looking for longer-term changes, and simply want to enter a position at a low price and exit that position months or between 1-2 years later at a higher price to take a profit. Trends are easy to estimate, but your estimations have no guarantee of being correct. For an uptrend, traders typically draw straight lines through the low points of the gyrations of the stock on the graph. This will help you estimate where the trend will end up at some future point in time. You can use this to set a selling point when you exit your position.

In the following chart, we see the trend in JNK from April through October.

Support and Resistance

Over relatively short time periods, stocks will stay confined between a range of prices. The low pricing point of this range is called support. The upper price point of the range is called resistance. The trader seeks to enter their position at a point of support. They can also place a stop loss order slightly below support so that they will exit the position if they bet wrong and share prices drop substantially. Then they can sell their stocks when the share price gets close to resistance levels, on the theory that it's more likely than not to drop back down after reaching resistance. The chart below illustrates this concept. Notice, however, that the stock eventually breaks out of the range. In this case, it's the support on the right side of the chart, and the price drops significantly.

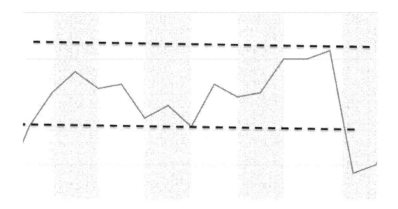

Candlesticks

A candlestick is a graphical representation of price and trading that occurred over a specified time period. Candlesticks have a body, and "wicks" sticking out of the ends. On most stock charts candlesticks are in color, with green representing a "bullish" candlestick and red representing a "bearish" candlestick. A bullish candlestick is a time period where buyers were moving into the market buying up shares. The bottom of the body indicates the opening price for the period, and the top of the body indicates the closing price.

A bearish candlestick represents a time period of decline in price. In this case, the top of the candlestick body is the opening price, and the bottom of the body is the closing price.

In either case, the top wick of a candlestick represents the high price throughout the time period. The bottom wick represents the low price for the time period. You can choose what time period you want to be represented, from one-minute out to one year. In the example below, we view the JNK chart but using candlesticks instead of a line. This is with one-day intervals. So the chart tells us whether or not it was a bullish or bearish day, and the sizes of the candlesticks indicate the spread in opening and closing prices for the day.

Traders will look for certain patterns in candlestick charts that indicate changing trends. For example, if the share price has been dropping for a long period, and a large bullish candlestick suddenly appears, that can indicate that buyers are now entering the market, pushing up prices. The trader will confirm the signal by looking up the volume of trading and comparing that to the average. A high-volume trading day is a strong indicator that the price will probably move up.

Alternatively, if the price is at peak value, and there is a bearish candlestick with higher than average volume, that tells us that traders are selling off their shares in droves, and a drop in price is probably coming.

Moving Averages

Another tool used in technical analysis is the moving average. A moving average is defined by the number of periods. So if we were using a chart that is framed in terms of days, a 9-period moving average would be a 9-day moving average. To plot points on the chart, the moving average would take the 9 previous days and average them. This helps eliminate noise from the stock charts and can be useful in spotting trends.

This example shows how a moving average (the purple line) generates a smooth curve for Apple, allowing us to focus more clearly on the trend in price.

The real benefit comes from comparing moving averages with different time periods. That's because it indicates that buyers are moving into the market more recently.

A simple moving average, one that simply calculates the average of the past given number of days, is going to give equal weight to prices days ago and prices more recently. This is an undesirable feature, and so traders prefer to use exponential moving averages to get more accurate data. Exponential moving averages weight the data, giving more weight to recent prices and less weight to more distant prices. Here is the Apple chart with a 9-day exponential moving average and a 20-day exponential moving average. The 20-day moving average is in red. Notice that when the 9-day moving average crosses above the 20-day moving average, the price enters an upward trend. Conversely, when the 9-day moving average passes below the 20-day moving average, the price enters a downward trend.

We also see signals in the candlesticks on the chart as well. Notice that at the low point in June, a larger green candlestick follows the red candlestick. That is a bearish day of selling Apple off was followed by a bullish day of rising prices. When a candlestick of one type is larger than the previous candlestick of the opposite type, we say that it engulfs the other candlestick. Usually, this is a sign of a trend reversal.

Chart Patterns

Traders also look for specific chart patterns that can indicate coming trend reversals. For example, you might be looking for signs that a stick is unable to move any higher in price after having undergone a large and long-lasting uptrend. What happens in these cases, is that the stock price will touch or reach a certain price level that is slightly higher than where it is at the present time, and do so two or more times. But each time it reaches the peak value, it will drop back down in price. That indicates that the stock has been bought up as much as it's going to be bought up at the present time. Traders also look for signals in the chart that a breakout is going to occur. A breakout can happen to the upside, that is, stock prices can increase a great deal, or it can happen to the downside, in which case a strong downward trend in share price will follow. In this case, you will see the price rise (or fall) and then for a short period of time, the trend will reverse. Then it reverts back to the same price rise (or decrease). This is a sign that the stock is "reverting to the mean," where the mean is the overall upward (or downward) trend. If you spot such a pattern early, it's possible to buy shares and be ready to profit from selling them when they reach the peak value.

Bollinger Bands

It's possible to utilize a wide array of more sophisticated tools. Bollinger bands attempt to combine the idea of a moving average with moving zones of support and resistance. The levels of support and resistance for a stock are calculated at any given time using the standard deviation. Bollinger bands will include a simple moving average curve in the center to represent the mean stock price. There will be upper and lower level curves, which show two-standard deviations from the mean. Here we see a chart of Apple using Bollinger bands:

For the time period shown, Bollinger bands provide a great deal of information. The mean share price for the period was $194.38, while the upper line, two standard deviations above the mean, was $206.05. The lower line, which is two standard deviations below the mean, is $182.71.

Knowing these values can be useful to some traders. For example, options traders that sell put options can use the values of the standard deviation to select their prices.

An Overview and Summary of Technical Analysis for the Stock Investor

Technical analysis does have its uses. However, unless you are a speculator, the use of technical analysis is questionable. Over the long term, the price movements shown on charts like these are not very important. If you are investing for the long term, dollar cost averaging is a more useful strategy. Think about the time horizons of your investments. If you are looking at 1-2 years, five years, or ten years, the momentary fluctuations shown here aren't very relevant. So focusing on the exact right moment to buy shares to save a penny is overkill. These charts are really only useful for speculators, that hope to profit for the sake of earning fast money rather than by investing in the companies themselves.

A second concern is a time spent doing this kind of analysis. Any time that you are spending doing technical analysis is the time that you are not spending doing fundamental analysis.

CHAPTER 6:

Consolidation Chart Patterns to Know

Many new traders who are first getting started with technical analysis often have a hard time seeing the less obvious signs that are pointing them towards various positions regarding their desired underlying assets which can lead to them missing out on key trades as the moment comes and goes without their notice. What these types of traders are often failing to take into account is that there is no single right way to trade which means you will want to learn about many different types of chart patterns if you hope to use technical analysis to bring in the profits you have always dreamed of. While there are countless types of technical indicators that you could consider, the following are the ones you should get familiar with first, before expanding your horizons as desired from there.

In order to ensure each effort is as effective as possible, however, you will want to ensure that you have a clear understanding of the benefits of the patterns you choose in addition to being familiar with their strengths and weaknesses.

A chart pattern is any one of a variety of different metrics with a value that is directly tied to the current price of an underlying asset. The goal of all chart patterns, then, is to show the direction the price of an underlying asset is going to move as well as what the extent of that movement is likely going to be. This is done through a mixture of analyzing past patterns and determining how and when they are going to repeat themselves in the future.

Instead, they are focused completely on price movement which makes them especially useful in the short-term and ends up losing some of their usefulness in the long-term as they typically lack the breadth of data that is required to be useful in long-term concerns. This then means that long-term investors are more likely to use technical indicators as a means of determining the right entry points to take advantage of, along with the right exit points to have in mind to avoid serious losses that were seriously preventable.

Flags and pennants

Both pennants and flags are signs of retracements or deviations from the existing trend that eventually become visible in the short term if viewed in comparison to the existing trend.

Retracements rarely lead to breakouts occurring in either direction, but the underlying asset likely won't be following the dominant trend in the first place so this shouldn't be much of an issue. However, the absence of a breakout will still result in a shorter trend overall.

The resistance and support lines of the pennant occur within a much larger overall trend before coming together to a point. A flag is quite similar, with the exception that its support and resistance lines come together in a parallel fashion instead.

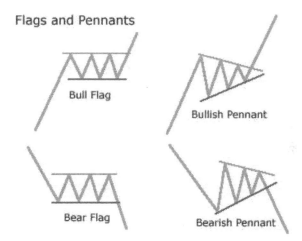

Pennants and flags are both more likely to be visible within the middle portion of the primary trend.

They also tend to last around two weeks on average before merging once again with the primary trend line. They are frequently associated with falling volume, which means that if you see a flag or pennant with volume that isn't dropping, then what you are likely really seeing is a reversal.

Head and shoulders

If you are looking for indicators of the length of a particular trend, then the head and shoulders formation of three peaks within the price chart tends to indicate an overall bearish pattern moving forward. The peaks to either side of the main peak should generally be a little small than the main peak which makes up the head. The price is the neckline in this scenario and when it reaches the right shoulder you can generally expect the price to drop off steeply.

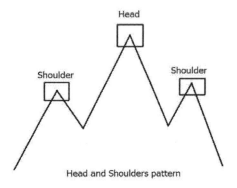

Head and Shoulders pattern

This formation most frequently occurs when a large group of traders ends up holding out for a final price increase after a long run of gains has already dropped most traders out of the running. If this occurs and the trend changes, then the price will fall and the head and shoulders will become visible. It is also possible for the opposite to appear in the form of a reverse head and shoulders. If you see this pattern then you can expect the price to soon be on the rise.

61

Cup with handle formation

This formation typically appears if a specific security reaches its peak price prior to dropping hard and fast for a prolonged period of time. Eventually, it is bound to rebound, however, which is when you want to go ahead and buy.

This is an indicator of a rapidly rising trend which means you are going to want to make an effort to take advantage of it as soon as possible if you want to avoid missing out.

The handle forms on the cup after those who initially purchased the security when it was at its previous high decide they can't wait any longer and begin to sell off their holdings.

This, in turn, causes new investors to become interested and then start to buy in. This formation rarely forms quickly, which means you should have plenty of time to act on it once it has started to form.

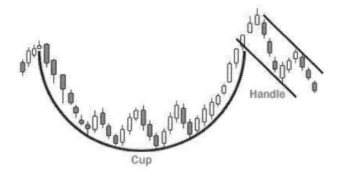

The best-case scenario here would be to take advantage of the details as soon as the handle starts to form to ensure that you have the greatest length of time possible to benefit from the change. If you see the cup and handle forming, you will still want to consider any other day to day patterns that may end up derailing the trend as they will go a long way towards determining its true effectiveness when it comes to buying at a given point.

Gann

While not universally trusted, Gann indicators have been used by traders for decades and remain a useful way of determining the direction a specific currency is likely to move next. Gann angles are used to determine certain elements of the chart include price, time and pattern which makes it easier to determine the future, past and even present of the market as well as how that information will determine the future of the price.

While you could be forgiven for thinking they are similar to trend lines, Gann angles are actually a different beast entirely. They are, in fact, a series of diagonal lines that move at a fixed rate and can likely be generated by your trading program. When they are compared to a trend line you will notice the Gann angle makes it possible for users to determine a true price at a specific point in the future assuming the current trend continues at its current strength.

If you compare a Gann angle to a trend line, then you will see that it makes it much easier to predict the likely movement of the price at a fixed point in the future.

This is not to say that it will always be accurate, but it can be useful when it comes to determining the location and relevant strength of a particular trend. As all times exist on the same line, the Gann angle can then also be used to predict resistance, direction strength and support as well as the timing on tops and bottoms.

Gann angles are most commonly used to determine the likely resistance and support as it only requires the trade to determine the right scale of the chart and then draw in the 1x2, 1x1 and 2x1 Gann angles from the primary bottoms to the tops. This makes it less complicated for the trader to frame the market, thus making it easier to determine the way the market is moving based on this predetermined framework. Positive trend angles indicate support in the market while negative trend angles indicate resistance. By understanding the angle on the chart, traders can more easily determine the most profitable times to buy and sell.

Additionally, it is important to always keep in mind the many ways that the market can move between various angles. If the market breaks from a single angle then it will likely move on towards the next, making your job to determine where it is likely headed next.

Support and resistance can also be found by combining the angles along with the horizontal lines. If you find that lots of angles appear to be clustering together near a specific price point, especially on a long-term chart, then you should be able to assume the resistance and support in that area is worth a closer look.

The 1x2 angle indicates that one unit of price moves for every two units of time, the 1x1 indicates that price and time move at the same rate and 2x1 indicates that two price units move for every single unit of time. Additional angles can be extrapolated following the same formula including 8x1, 4x1, 1x4 and 1x8.

When it comes to performing this type of analysis it is important to always use the proper scale which is a square chart whereby the 1x1 angle moves at an angle of 45 degrees. This is a test then as only when the chart is scaled properly will the angle appear appropriately.

Ascending triangle

This pattern typically forms during an upward trend and indicates that the current pattern is going to continue.

It is a bullish pattern that says greater growth and volume are on the way. It can also be formed during a reversal, signaling the end to a downward trend.

Ascending Triangle Formation

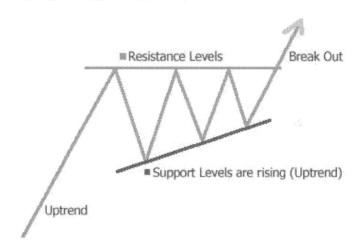

Triple bottom

The triple bottom, named for the 3 bottoming out points of a given stock, tends to indicate that a reversal is on the way. You can tell a triple bottom by the fact that the price rebounds to the same point after each period of bottoming out. After the third period, it is likely to reverse the trend by breaking out.

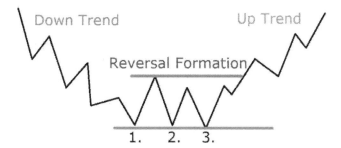

Descending triangle

This is similar to the ascending triangle but is bearish rather than bullish. It indicates that the current downward trend is likely to continue. It can occasionally be seen during a reversal but is much more likely to be a continuation.

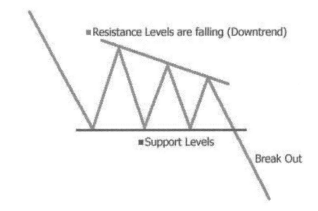

Inverse head and shoulders

The inverse head and shoulders consists of 3 low points always returning to the same higher price. The lowest point is considered the head while the shoulders are a pair of low points that are equal to one another. After the second shoulder, a breakout is likely to occur that will pick up volume as it goes.

Bullish triangle

This is a symmetrical triangle pattern that can be easily determined by a pair of trend lines that converge at a point. The lower trend line tracks support while the upper tracks resistance. Once the price breaks through the upper line then you know that a breakout has occurred that will rapidly pick up both steam and volume.

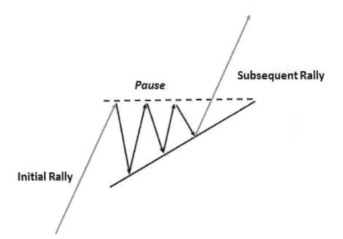

CHAPTER 7:

Relationship with Fundamental Analysis

Fundamental Analysis

In order to trade in the forex market successfully, one of the most important things you can learn is the most reliable way to spot a trade that is going to end up being reliably profitable from one that blows up in your face. This is where proper analysis comes in handy, whether technical or fundamental. Fundamental analysis is easier to learn, though it is more time consuming to use properly, while technical analysis can be more difficult to wrap your mind around but can be done quite quickly once you get the hang of it. While both will help you to find the information you are looking for, they go about doing so in different ways; fundamental analysis concerns itself with looking at the big picture while technical analysis focuses on the price of a given currency in the moment to the exclusion of all else.

This divide when it comes to information means that fundamental analysis will always be useful when it comes to determining currencies that are currently undervalued based on current market forces. The information that is crucial to fundamental analysis is generated by external sources which means there won't always be new information available at all times.

Generally speaking, fundamental analysis allows you a likely glimpse at the future of the currency in question based on a variety of different variables such as publicized changes to the monetary policy that the countries you are interested in might affect. Fundamental analysis is always made up of the same set of steps which are described in detail below.

Start by determining the baseline: When it comes to considering the fundamental aspects of a pair of currencies, the first thing that you are going to want to do is to determine a baseline from which those currencies tend to return to time and again compared to the other commonly traded currency pairs. This will allow you to determine when it is time to make a move as you will be able to easily pinpoint changes to the pair that are important enough to warrant further consideration.

In order to accurately determine the baseline, the first thing you will need to do is to look into any relevant macroeconomic policies that are currently affecting your currency of choice. You will also want to look into the available historical data as past behavior is one of the best indicators of future events. While this part of the process can certainly prove tedious, their importance cannot be overstated.

After you have determined the historical precedent of the currency pair you are curious about, the next thing you will want to consider is the phase the currency is currently in and how likely it is going to remain in that phase for the foreseeable future. Every currency goes through phases on a regular basis as part of the natural market cycle.

The first phase is known as the boom phase which can be easily identified by its low volatility and high liquidity. The opposite of this phase is known as the bust phase wherein volatility is extremely high, and liquidity is extremely low. There are also pre and post versions of both phases that can be used to determine how much time the phase in question has before it is on its way out. Determining the right phase is a key part of knowing when you are on the right track regarding a particular trading pair.

In order to determine the current major or minor phase, the easiest thing to do is to start by checking the current rates of defaults along with banks loans as well as the accumulated reserve levels of the currencies in question. If numbers are relatively low them a boom phase is likely to be on its way, if not already in full swing. If the current numbers have already overstayed their welcome, then you can be fairly confident that a post-boom phase is likely to start at any time. Alternatively, if the numbers in question are higher than the baseline you have already established then you know that the currency in question is either due for a bust phase or is already experiencing it.

You can make money from either of the major phases as long as you are aware of them early on enough to turn a profit before things start to swing back in the opposite direction. Generally speaking, this means that the faster you can pinpoint what the next phase is going to be, the greater your dividends of any related trades will be.

Broaden your scope: After you have a general idea of the baseline for your favored currencies, as well as their current phases, the next thing you will need to do is look at the state of the global market as a whole to determine how it could possibly affect your trading pair. To ensure this part of the process is as effective as possible you are going to need to look beyond the obvious signs that everyone can see to find the indicators that you know will surely make waves as soon as they make it into the public consciousness.

One of the best places to start looking for this information is in the technology sector as emerging technologies can turn entire economies around in a relatively short period of time.

Technological indicators are often a great way to take advantage of a boom phase by getting in on the ground floor as, once it starts, it is likely to continue for as long as it takes for the technology to be fully integrated into the mainstream. Once it reaches the point of complete saturation then a bust phase is likely going to be on the horizon, and sooner rather than later. If you feel as though the countries responsible for the currencies in question are soon going to be in a post-boom or post-bust phase, then you are going to want to be very careful in any speculative market as the drop-off is sure to be coming and it is difficult to pinpoint exactly when.

If you know that a phase shift is coming, but you aren't quite sure when, then it is a good idea to focus on smaller leverage amounts than during other phases as they are more likely to pay off in the short-term. At the same time, you are also going to want to keep any eye out for long-term positions that are likely to pay out if a phase shift does occur. On the other hand, if the phase you are in currently is just starting out, you can make trades that have a higher potential for risk as the time concerns aren't going to be nearly serious enough to warrant the additional caution.

Look to global currency policy: While regional concerns are often going to be able to provide you with an insight into some long-reaching changes a given currency might experience in the near future, you are also going to want to broaden your search, even more, to include relevant global policies as well. While determining where you are going to start can be difficult at first, all you really need to do is to provide the same level of analysis that you used at the micro level on a macro basis instead. The best place to start with this sort of thing is going to be with the interest rates of the major players including the Federal Reserve, the European Central Bank, the Bank of Japan, the Bank of England and any other banks that may affect the currencies you are considering trading.

You will also need to consider any relevant legal mandates or policy biases that are currently in play to make sure that you aren't blindsided by these sorts of things when the times actually comes to stop doing research and actually make a move. While certainly time consuming, understanding every side of all the major issues will make it far easier to determine if certain currencies are flush with supply where the next emerging markets are likely to appear and what worldwide expectations are when it comes to future interest rate changes as well as market volatility.

Don't forget the past: Those who forget the past are doomed to repeat it and that goes double for forex traders. Once you have a solid grasp on the current events of the day, you are going to want to dig deeper and look for scenarios in the past that match what is currently going on today. This level of understanding will ultimately lead to a greater understanding of the current strength of your respective currencies while also giving you an opportunity to accurately determine the length of the current phase as well.

In order to ensure you are able to capitalize on your knowledge as effectively as possible, the ideal time to jump onto a new trade is going to be when one of the currency pairs is entering a post-boom phase while the other is entering the post-bust phase. This will ensure that the traditional credit channels are not exhausted completely, and you will thus have access to the maximum amount of allowable risk of any market state. This level of risk is going to start dropping as soon as the market conditions hit an ideal state and will continue until the situation with the currencies is reversed so getting in and making a profit when the time is right is crucial to your long-term success.

Don't forget volatility: Keeping the current level of volatility in mind is crucial when it comes to ensuring that the investments you are making are actually going to pay off in a reasonable period of time. Luckily, it is relatively easy to determine the current level of volatility in a given market, all you need to do is to look to that country's stock market. The greater the level of stability the market in question is experiencing, the more confident those who are investing in it are going to remain when means the more stable the forex market is going to remain as well.

Additionally, it is important to keep in mind that, no matter what the current level of volatility may be, the market is never truly stable. As such, the best traders are those who prepare for the worst while at the same time hoping for the best. Generally speaking, the more robust a boom phase is, the lower the overall level of volatility is going to be.

Think outside the box on currency pairs: All of the information that you gather throughout the process should give you a decent idea regarding the current state of the currency pairs you are keeping tabs on.

CHAPTER 8:

Range Trading or Channel Trading

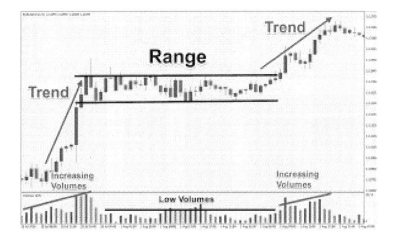

R ange bound strategy is also known as the average accurate range indicator (ATR). This is one of the favorite indicators with so many users. Range bounder strategy is an indicator that measures volatility in the forex market. You need to know that the ATR indicator DOES not tell you the direction of the trend. Meaning that the market value may be higher; however, the ATR value may below. ATR indicators only measure volatility; thus, it focuses more on the range of the candles. So as the scope of the candles gets smaller, the indicator values will decrease.

You, therefore, need to find explosive breakout trade before. You need to know that the market is always changing so it will move. It will run from a period of low volatility to a period of high volatility. It will then move from a period of high volatility to a period of low volatility. Thus a range bond strategy is more of a cycle, and it continues. This is how the market will move. Therefore if you have noticed that the market is in a low volatility environment, then there is a good chance that volatility could expand soon.

Once you have learned the circle, then it's time to pull out your ATR indicators by paying attention to your ATR value. Especially the multi-year ATR low value. You will notice that there is a point when the market is weak, and the volatility will be as well when the market breaks down, volatility picks up. You need to note that when a market breaks down, there may be a big move that may follow. This is a powerful trading technique that helps understand your market.

You also need to know how to set up a proper trade loss. This is where the trade indicator becomes so useful. Often traders will look at price rejection level help them know how much buffer they should put as your stop loss to prevent you from being stopped out prematurely. Once this is done, you need to know how to ride massive trends in the market using the ATR indicator. Get your ATR value and make sure that you use the multiple of that value to trailing your stop loss.

An ATR indicator should also help predict market reversal. You need to note that an ATR indicator is a potential energy tool. Thus, if you look at the indicator and it tells that throughout the past three weeks its 300 pips, based on the prior period. So the energy that has been stocked for a week has been used up. Thus the market could show signs of reversing from there. Accordingly, this value will alert you of what to expect.

Sometimes a stock will repeatedly swing between two pricing levels for a relatively extended period of time. That is, it is trading within a range. The range can be estimated by drawing levels of support and resistance on the same chart.

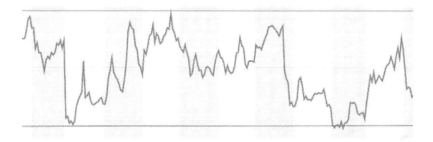

In the above chart, the price level of resistance is indicated by the upper red line. The price level for support is indicated by the lower, purple line. Ranges can last for any length of time, and can even go on for months. The key to finding a trading range is that it lasts over a time frame that is of interest in your particular case. Remember that trade ranges don't last forever, at some point there will be a breakout to the upside or the downside, and the stock will settle in with a new level of support and/or resistance. These are guidelines only.

Trading Strategy for Ranges

However, notice that the price fluctuations within the range offer opportunities for profit. Once you have established a level of support, you can use that as your price level to enter the position.

It's possible that you will miss out on the upside, but a smart trader takes a methodical approach. Rather than being greedy or waiting around to see if the price might continue increasing, the smart trader sets up rules for their trade beforehand, and they stick to their rules. It's better to ensure a limited profit and duplicate the process, than it is to wait too long hoping for higher highs and find yourself losing money. Unfortunately that happens all too often.

CHAPTER 9:

News Trading

News Trading. Again, this is where you will want to be paying attention to the happenings of the financial world. When big news hits regarding a stock that you are informed enough about that you are able to generally predict its market moves, take advantage of the moment by buying or selling. This should usually be done very early in the day, shortly after the market opens up since that is when the news usually will first come out. If you wait until later in the day, everyone will have gotten a feel for how the market is reacting and thus may not be so eager to sell or buy. The day trader's objective, however, is to take advantage of small, yet drastic moves within the market, and so buying or selling when the market is at its most volatile may be of the most use to you. It is important to remember not to get ahead of yourself though. Be sure to think through each trade calmly and rationally, avoiding making any passionate decisions that you may later pay through the teeth for.

A word of warning however: there is a difference between news trading, which is legal, and trading on information that you already know ahead of the market. If, for example, a friend tells you that tomorrow morning company XYZ is going to file for bankruptcy, you would be tempted to immediately sell your stock for a hefty profit before it collapses. But to do so before the company announced it would indicate illegal activity. Similarly, if you decide to scalp (different from the first strategy), then you are purposely talking up or down a particular security causing the market to change and then taking advantage of it. That would also be viewed as unfavorable by authorities. Don't do it.

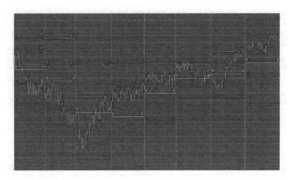

Other Trading Strategies

Since you have now learned the basics of day trading, let us take a look at some of the more artistic aspects. These strategies are only a few of those available and will work differently for each individual depending upon mindset, experience, and confidence. Some of these strategies are old and time-proven, but as always, they can be subject to change in order to fit a specific trader. Peruse these few options and take into consideration which ones might be the best fit for you in terms of capital, how much daily time you can commit to trading, and your current comfort level.

Scalping. This is probably the easiest for traders who don't want to put any significant amount of money on the line, but it requires a lot of patience and fast work. Essentially, scalping involves acquiring very small increments of cash, usually in pence, and slowly accumulating it by making numerous small trades a day. It relies upon the bid-ask spread, in which the bid is how much buyers are willing to pay for a security and then ask is how much sellers require for someone else to purchase it. In order to make a profit, traders are looking for when the gap between the bid and ask is slightly wider or narrower than usual. In the case of a wider spread, there will be a higher demand to buy than sell, and so traders will attempt to sell off their securities for slightly more pence than the normal ask price.

If the bid-ask spread is narrower, there is a greater demand to sell than buy, so that the prices will be slightly lower to buy a security. In this case, a trader will purchase a security at a lower price and then sell it again when the bid-ask spread has returned to normal levels.

Be sure to speak with your broker and ensure you are making enough money scalping so that you don't end up spending all of your profits paying commission.

Momentum Trading. This is where all of the constant reviewing of the financial world will come in hand. Momentum trading is when a trader buys or sells a stock that is on an extremely volatile upswing or downswing. Where all of the research comes in is that you need to be absolutely sure that your stock is truly on a momentum and will not reverse itself after you have already made your move. Confirm this by reviewing charts and finding where that stock has hit its highest and lowest points. If the stock you are looking at is not going to make a move more sufficient than it's normal peaks and valleys then it is not worth your time. In addition to this, reading financial news about changes in companies and emerging partnerships will also be good indicators of a stock entering a period of high volatility.

To complete a momentum trade, you will need to chart the trends of the particular stock you are interested in and, when you believe it is going to hit momentum, wait for a gap and then enter your trade. Give the stock most of the day to breathe so that you can reap all of the benefits of the momentum (and your game plan for this particular stock and strategy should reflect that) before exiting. As always, don't forget to place your stop-loss order as soon as you enter the trade.

Pivot Points. With the help of an abundance of charts, this particular strategy is a fairly easy one to grasp. Essentially, pivot points take advantage of the highs and lows of the day. Since you should be dealing with most of the same stocks day in and day out, you will be able to chart the highs and lows of each particular stock over the long term. However, you will not have this added advantage when you begin day trading, so it is advisable to review past daily charts.

In order to take advantage of this strategy, mark out the highs and lows and then watch the daily charts like a hawk to find where you believe the lowest or highest point is. Once you have identified that point, buy or sell as is appropriate in order to gain a profit. In the case of buying, your profit will come from an exceptionally low price. In the case of selling, you will want to sell a stock for an astronomically higher price than you bought it. Take a look at the graph above to get an idea of when to buy a stock. Note that the "R's" labelled on the graph represent resistance within the market (typed in green) and the "S's" represent support (typed in red). Although this is actually a depiction of the first 8 months on the Dow Jones in 2009, it is easy to see how looking at a daily, monthly, or yearly chart would help you to determine the average highs and lows of a particular stock. Theoretically, in this case you would have wanted to buy the stock at the very lowest point on the chart and then sell it at the highest point, which may or may not be represented on this graph. However, since this is day trading and you are only dealing in the short-term, you will want to close out your position by the end of the day.

As you can see, the strategies involved in day trading really aren't that difficult to grasp. Unlike options trading, they rely on a few basic principles and are flexible to almost everyone's needs. Where they get difficult is when traders must keep track of multiple trades at the same time and not get them confused. Doing so can often lead to disaster in which the trader forgets to make his or her exit and then loses money on what would have otherwise been a profitable trade. Avoid this by keeping a proper log of your trades in your journal and don't take on more than you can handle. Study up on more strategies, as these are just the top of the iceberg, and find which works with best with your trading style and will reap you the greatest reward.

CHAPTER 10:

Pairs Trading

Currency Pairs

In the Forex, the value of one currency is only relevant when compared to another, which is why we talk about currency pairs.

The currency that is used as the reference is called the base currency; the money that is quoted, concerning the base currency, is instead called "quoted" or "secondary."

In the case of the Euro/Dollar pair, written Eur/Usd, the currency on the left is the Base currency, so in this case, the Euro, and the quoted currency is on the right, in this example the Dollar.

Therefore, the price of the Eur/Usd quotation tells us how many units of the quoted currency are needed to buy one unit of the base currency.

Let's see a quick example:

Very simply, if the current price of Eur/Usd is 1.10897, it means that 1€ corresponds to 1.10897$.

The term Long or Buy indicates the purchase of a pair of currencies in which we assume a rise in prices, thus focusing on the increase in the value of the base currency and therefore on a weakening of the currency quoted.

With the term Short or Sell, we mean instead the sale of a currency pair, in which we assume a fall in prices, so we expect a decline from the base currency.

Let us take a case where the Euro/Dollar pair's current quotation price is 1.10. This means that 1€ equals 1.10$.

If at this point we open a Buy operation, and the price subsequently rises from 1.10 to 1.20, it means that at this point 1€ is equivalent to 1.20$, so the value of the Euro against the dollar has increased: you need more dollars to have 1€ and, consequently, we are in profit because we have opened a bullish operation, called Buy or Long.

On the contrary, always assuming the quotation 1.10 as the current starting price, we decide to open a transaction Sell: then, betting on a fall in prices, i.e. a devaluation of the base currency, we will gain if the price goes down from 1.10.

If then the price goes down to 1.05, we will be in profit. Conversely, if the price should rise above the threshold of 1.10 (for example to 1.15), we would better be selling or we will be losing money.

Further, we will see how profit is calculated based on price movements.

In the meantime, I hope we have understood that the relationship between two currencies is called currency pair. These pairs can be divided into three macro-categories:

- Major Pairs.
- Minor Pairs (or Cross).
- Exotic Pairs.

Major Pairs

Major or significant pairs are all major currency pairs that contain the US dollar, either as a base currency or as a quoted currency.

These pairs generate the most trading activity on the currency market. The main features of these significant pairs are higher liquidity and lower spreads.

The most frequent pair traded in absolute is the Euro/Dollar with 28% of total transactions, followed immediately by the pair Dollar/Yen with 14% of the transactions.

Minor Pairs

Minor pairs, also called cross currency pairs, are all those currency pairs that do not contain the U.S. dollar.

Exotic Pairs

Exotic currency pairs are all those in which there is the dollar combined with other international currencies that are not among the top 7. These pairs are much less traded: they have low liquidity and therefore involve a high spread.

Asset Class

There are different perspectives you can take when classifying asset classes. It would be perfectly valid for instance to say that the main asset classes are stocks, bonds, currencies and commodities. For most market participants, that way of looking at asset classes makes the most sense.

But for systematic, quantitative traders, another definition may be more practical. When looking at the various markets we have available to us, we can group them in different ways. One way to group asset classes would be to look at the type of instruments used to trade them. The type of instrument is, for a systematic trader, often more important than the properties of the underlying market.

This becomes particularly clear with futures, as we will soon see, where you can trade just about anything in a uniform manner. Futures behave quite differently than stocks, from a mechanical point of view, and that's important when building trading models.

The currency space is an interesting demonstration of this concept. You can trade spot currencies, or you can trade currency futures. It's really the same underlying asset, but the mechanics of the two types of instruments is very different and would need to be modeled in different ways.

CHAPTER 11:

Intraday Scalping

Intraday and Multiday Operations

We have seen before that the principal trades are: scalper, day trading (or intraday), multiday, and position.

We are mainly interested in intraday and multiday trading: this is because, usually, we retailers do not have tools advanced enough that we can operate in the scalping world with a certain speed of execution, and we cannot open a trade and wait for months before closing it. If you want to try these two transactions on your own, of course, I have nothing to object to.

So, we're going to analyze the intraday and multiday trades. We choose above all these two because, given my quantitative analyses, there are a higher number of cases to be investigated and therefore data closer to expectations.

Let's use an example: if I analyze the past ten years of the Euro Dollar (EurUsd), studying an intraday strategy, I can have thousands of executed trades to explain the trends; unlike a "position" strategy in which there would be much fewer trades, consequently, this means less statistical predictability.

Intraday

As we have said, intraday or day trading includes all those transactions that are opened, managed, and closed in a day.

This means that if I open a Long operation (i.e., assuming a rise in prices) at 10:00 in the morning, then I will manage it and usually close it within 24 hours.

My automatic systems are mainly intraday or at the closest after 24/48h: this is because I like seeing activities open, managed, and closed within the day.

I prefer this type of operation also because I can use quantitative analyses; there is a need to study past years' strategies with a good number of trades.

Let's take, for example, the time frame of the last ten years: in the case of position strategies, we could hypothetically have 20 to 50 trades to analyze. How do I know, then, whether this is a real statistical advantage or whether it is mere luck?

It is a different ballgame to have 1,000/2,000/3,000 trades to analyze: with a larger pool of data you can better evaluate the strategy and type of operation. You will never be sure that past studies will be reflected identically in the future, but yes, you can rely on a more accurate analysis.

But it is not enough to have a large number of trades to analyze: an ad hoc procedure is also needed to avoid significant assessment errors. All of which I will explain in more detail in the training courses I have created and which I will tell you about later.

Another advantage of closing trades within the day is to avoid sudden increases in spreads in the transition from the current stock exchange day to the next day, when there is a transfer of liquidity that involves an increase in ranges and that risks going to hit a Stop Loss set, thus creating the potential of finding unpleasant losses on your account. We will see in more detail what is meant by Stop Loss and Take Profit.

A small disadvantage of the intraday operation is having daily "costs of management." For daily costs, we mean the spread and the commissions managed from the broker that we use: but we will see this in detail.

In addition to this, it must be said that, obviously, in intraday transactions, the gain is "limited." Limited in the sense that, objectively, we cannot make significant gains from a single intraday trade, as it could happen for a long-term trade kept open for months. This is because price movements are usually never so large as to allow for high pay-outs, except for the case of macroeconomic news that have a significant impact on the market and make prices jump enormously. But these events are now quite rare.

Multiday

Multiday trading is a fair trade-off between intraday and long-term trading.

The main advantage of this operation is, above all, being able to ride the trend for several days when we are in position, and the market is giving us reason to: this, therefore, turns into a higher gain, a cold pressing of the asset of reference.

All this with the help of techniques such as breakeven or trailing profit (trade management tools in progress), which allow you to make the operation safe by setting a minimum level of profit.

However, I would advise you to close your operations on Friday evening, before the market closes. This is because on Monday, at the reopening of the trading sessions, you can find yourself in front of significant gaps in the market and very high spreads, which can also result in premature closures of operations caused by the activation of the stop loss. I mean, you could end up with unpleasant surprises.

At the end of this paragraph, dedicated to the various operations, I can undoubtedly say that none excludes the other and that on an excellent diversification, any type of trading can be used, except scalping.

With a long-term analysis, you can include position strategies in your portfolio: for example, if you believe that Amazon will grow in the next few years, devote a portion of your capital to this, wait for a retracement of prices and purchases assuming a rise.

For intraday and multiday trading, you can use trading systems, both for analysis and for live trading after adequate studies, and with the right methodology and useful tools.

CHAPTER 12:

Breakout

Break out is known to be one of the most straightforward approaches to use in forex trading. It is easy to note when you are wrong. You can tell when the price goes higher the range or lower your range. Break up is defined either by the swing high or swing lows or characterized by support or resistance. Swing low is a mini version of support and resistance. They are not of significance, but they are pretty evident on the chats when you identify swing highs or lows in the market. Resistance in the market is where there will be potential sellers coming into the market. Resistance is much more respectable and is vary obviously in your chat.

There is a period that you should avoid trading breakouts. You need to know that you should not trade breakouts against the trends as you know that the trend is not your "friend" until it bends. It is not much you can gain if you are trading against the trend. You should also not trade breakouts when the market is far much from the stricture. The problem of going longs in the structure is that you will never know where to put your stop loss as there will know structure to guide you.

To trade breakouts like a pro, you need to:

- Trade with the trend

- Trade near the stricture

- Trade breakouts with the buildups. Buildups are the congested area in your chat where the sellers are not making any pressure. Maybe it is due to sellers not being there, or there are a good number of buyers who are willing to buy at higher prices. These are signs of strengths that you need to look up to.

Breakout Strategy

This is a common strategy employed by traders new and old. The main idea behind this strategy is that you chose a price point for a given stock that, once hit, will indicate enough of a positive swing to justify buying more of the stock. When using this method, it is important to consider a price point as well as the amount of time you are willing to give the stock in order for it to reach that price point. This is a strong strategy to employ if the market is moving in a certain direction and ensures you will always know when to jump on the bandwagon.

This strategy is an effective choice if the market is currently or was recently at either a drastic high or low.

To complete this strategy properly, all you need to do is set an order that is either above the high or slightly above the low and then play the averages. If the market is not moving strongly in one direction or another, then this strategy can easily backfire as prices are more likely to stick to prescribed ranges. If there are no strong signs of trending use with caution.

Retracement strategy

To properly implement this strategy, it is important that you are able to determine a likely pattern for the price of the stock to continue trending towards. To take advantage of this fact, you wait for each price increase before the inevitable decrease which comes as some people sell and others try and trade the opposite.

You sell on the high and use the profits to buy back in at an increase of shares under the assumption that it will rise again. Then you simply repeat until you are no longer sure of the increase.

This strategy will only work effectively when there is something major enough to cause ripples across the market that are not felt all at once. This strategy will become less effective the unsure you are about additional jumps in price and should therefore always be used carefully.

You may be tempted after seeing a single large jump from a stock to try and employ this strategy but beware of using it flippantly. Stay strong and you will turn a profit.

Pivot points

In order to take advantage of this strategy, it is important that you first become extremely familiar with the specific securities that you prefer to work with day in and day out so that you have a general understanding of their high and low points, thus making it easier to predict where it is likely they are going to go next.

If you don't have access to this type of first-hand information, then you can use existing historical charts to make do, as long as you can clearly determine the highs and lows for the security in question. In order to ensure this strategy works as well as possible, you will need to have a clear top and bottom determined. You will then simply buy or sell based on not where the security is currently going, but where it is likely to go once it rounds the pivot point and starts back the other way.

Essentially, you are going to look at these charts and try to figure out where the lowest and the highest points are. When the stock gets to the lowest point, it is time to enter the market and purchase the stock at a lower price, hopefully, lower than market value. You will then hold onto the stock for a bit, waiting for it to reach the high point on the chart, or at least higher than where you started so that you can make a profit when it's time to sell.

Pairs trading

As the name implies, pairs trading is a strategy wherein you choose a general category of stocks, tech stocks, for example, and then go short on one stock in the sector while going long on the other. Making these trades at the same time will bolster your odds of ensuring one of them actually turns a profit while also ensuring that you are able to turn a profit regardless of the conditions in the market. You will also be able to see movement on all sides more easily including sideways movement, downtrends, and uptrends and then bet on a few different options within the market. Since you are betting on both sides, you are more likely to make some money compared to just picking one kind of stock.

Contrarian trading

Day traders that use momentum to trade will buy bonds and stocks when their prices are going up and selling them when the prices begin to go down. These people believe that if something is going up in its price, it will continue to do so for a while and that something that is falling will continue to fall. Momentum trading is only one trading strategy, and, for most traders, it works well, especially with a strong bull market.

Contrarian trading, though, is the exact opposite of those momentum traders, and it also has the possibility to work very well. The belief in the contrarian strategy is that things aren't going to continue to rise forever and that nothing will fall forever.

The contrarian investment style goes against the market trends that are currently prevailing by purchasing assets that are performing poorly, and sell them once they are performing well. This type of investor believes that when another person says that the market is moving up, does so when they are completely invested and aren't planning on purchasing more. This means the market is at its peak, which means a downturn is about to happen, and the contrarian investor has already sold.

A trader that uses the contrarian strategy will look for assets that have been on the rise and will sell them, and they prefer to buy stocks that have been falling in price. It doesn't mean that you should buy cheap or sell but instead look for things that appear to be overpriced and to buy what looks to be a bargain. Contrarian investment also places emphasis on out-of-favor securities that have a low P/E ratio.

This investment style is distinguished from others in that they buy and sell against the grain of what other investors believe at a given time. These investors will enter the market when others feel pessimistic about it, and its value is a lot lower than the intrinsic value. When there is such a largely pessimistic view about a stock, the chances of the price lowering so low that the risks and downfalls of the stock are overblown. Finding out which of the distressed stocks to purchase and then sell it after the company has recovered will boost the value of the stock. This is the main play of the contrarian investor.

CHAPTER 13:

Application on the Options Market

Very successful investor says that research makes all the difference not only in options trading but trading in general. The better resources you have the more knowledge you will acquire. This is especially significant for learning as much as you can about underlying securities for example or to find as many details about the market that is constantly changing. Significance of the right source of information eventually becomes the key to your progress, even more, if the world of options trading is still new to you. We can say that there are two types of relevant resources for options trading. The first one includes traditional resources such as magazines, newsletters, and newspapers. The second type is newer, it has a variety of options and these kinds of resources are mostly referred to as online resources.

The Internet offers a variety of free content, which is why many investors see it as their first stop whenever they need some kind of information. Further technology development also had a huge impact on the amount of information, tools, and possibilities that a person can access so using apps for education and trading, in general, has become a common thing. In the following text, we will list some of the most relevant option trading resources divided into the categories we explained above.

Even though they are considered to be more traditional, magazines, newspapers, newsletters, are still popular for research, for both experienced investors and beginners on the market. It is useful to know that many newsletters offer paid services such as recommendations, picks, research of certain categories and other relevant information.

We will start with the magazines. Some of them such as Forbes is still one of the greatest and strongest magazines in the world for this matter. So, we have Fortune, Forbes, Consumer Money Adviser, Bloomberg BusinessWeek, Kiplinger's, and Fast Company as some of the most relevant magazines today.

Newspapers that you might find useful are the Financial Times, the Wall Street Journal, The Washington Post, Value Line, and Barron's.

Some of the most recommended ones are ETF Trader, Market Watch Options Trader, The Proactive Fund Investor, Hulbert Interactive, The Technical Indicator, The Prudent Speculator, Dow Theory Forecasts, and Global Resources Trading

When it comes to online resources, they are probably the most frequent source of information for everything, not only for options trading. However, it is possible to find numerous websites that offer research that is up to date. Many of these analyses and other useful data can be found for free.

Technology development made many things easier with trading. Many apps have emerged and enabled investors to keep a close track of their investments at all times. It is important to know that there are apps that are not only for investment but for brokerage companies too. In the following text, you can find some of the investment apps that are most frequently used and that have excellent feedback.

How to avoid costly mistakes

Losing profit is not something that you want as an investor since the main purpose of options trading is to make money not the other way around. To do so, some tips can help you avoid mistakes that can be costly.

First of all, don't invest more capital than you are ready to lose. Keep in mind that trading options don't go without risks. There aren't any guarantees that the propositions that you'll face with will gain you anything and your decisions are based on the hunch. Furthermore, if you don't have good timing and your hunch isn't right, you can lose the entire investment, not only the cash you were expecting to earn. The best way to avoid this kind of scenario is to start small. It is recommended that you use no more than 15 percent of your total portfolio on options trading.

The second tip that you should be aware of at all times is that good research gets the job done. If somebody says that it is a good idea to invest in options and you rush in and make an order without thinking it through, once more, you can lose more than you could earn. You should make your own research and decide based on facts before you start trading.

There is another thing that you should be mindful of. No matter the strategy you choose for options trading, you should always try to adjust it to the current condition on the market. Not all strategies work in all environments which is why you must be up to date with circumstances in the world of finance and you have to adapt accordingly.

Without a proper exit strategy, it is useless to talk about successful business in options trading. You need to make a plan that you will follow through regardless of your emotions. Rational decisions are the main factor in trade, being emotional and making fast decisions out of rage or spite or feeling of insecurity can only make things worse. Stick to the plan you figured before you started trading because it should have both downside and upside points along with the timeframe for its execution. Just like you shouldn't let negative feelings influence your decision making, you shouldn't allow the feeling of over-confidence in gaining large profits pull you back from the path you have set for yourself.

When it comes to risks, there is no need to take more risks than necessary, which means that the level of risk should be as big as your comfort with it. Level of risk tolerance is different for everyone; it is an individual think and only the investor himself can set its limit. Try to estimate that level and then choose all further actions accordingly. It is the safest premise to base your decisions on without being too insecure about every choice you make.

CHAPTER 14:

Analyzing Mood Swing in the Market

T he market is a chaotic place with a number of traders vying for dominance over one another. There are a countless number of strategies and time frames in play and at any point, it is close to impossible to determine who will emerge with the upper hand. In such an environment, how is it then possible to make any money? After all, if everything is unpredictable, how can you get your picks right?

Well, this is where thinking in terms of probabilities comes into play. While you cannot get every single bet right, as long as you get enough right and make enough money on those to offset your losses, you will make money in the long run.

It's not about getting one or two right. It's about executing the strategy with the best odds of winning over and over again and ensuring that your math works out with regards to the relationship between your win rate and average win.

So, it really comes down to finding patterns which repeat themselves over time in the markets. What causes these patterns? Well, the other traders of course! To put it more accurately, the orders that the other traders place in the market are what creates patterns that repeat themselves over time.

The first step to understanding these patterns is to understand what trends and ranges are. Identifying them and learning to spot when they transition into one another will give you a massive leg up not only with your options trading but also with directional trading.

Trends

In theory spotting a trend is simple enough. Look left to right and if the price is headed up or down, it's a trend. Well, sometimes it is really that simple. However, for the majority of the time you have both with and counter-trend forces operating in the market. It is possible to have long counter trend reactions within a larger trend and sometimes, depending on the time frame you're in, these counter-trend reactions take up the majority of your screen space.

Trend vs. Range

This is a chart of the UK100 CFD, which mimics the FTSE 100, on the four-hour time frame. Three-quarters of the chart is a downtrend and the last quarter is a wild uptrend. Using the looking left to right guideline, we'd conclude that this instrument is in a range. Is that really true though?

Just looking at that chart, you can clearly see that short-term momentum is bullish. So, if you were considering taking a trade on this, would you implement a range strategy or a trending one? This is exactly the sort of thing that catches traders up.

The key to deciphering trends is to watch for two things: counter trend participation quality and turning points. Let's tackle counter trend participation first.

Counter Trend Participation

When a new trend begins, the market experiences extremely imbalanced order flow which is tilted towards one side. There's isn't much counter trend participation against this seeming tidal wave of with trend orders. Price marches on without any opposition and experiences only a few hiccups.

As time goes on though, the trend forces run out of steam and have to take breaks to gather themselves. This is where counter trend traders start testing the trend and trying to see how far back into the trend they can go. While it is unrealistic to expect a full reversal at this point, the quality of the correction or pushback tells us a lot about the strength distribution between the with and counter-trend forces.

Eventually, the counter-trend players manage to push so far back against the trend that a stalemate results in the market. The counter-trend forces are equally balanced and thus the trend comes to an end. After all, you need an imbalance for the market to tip one way or another and a balanced order flow is only going to result in a sideways market.

While all this is going on behind the scenes, the price chart is what records the push and pull between these two forces. Using the price chart, we can not only anticipate when a trend is coming to an end but also how long it could potentially take before it does. This second factor, which helps us estimate the time it could take, is invaluable from an options perspective, especially if you're using a horizontal spread strategy.

In all cases, the greater the number of them, the greater the counter-trend participation in the market. The closer a trend is to ending, the greater the counter-trend participation. Thus, the minute you begin to see price move into a large, sideways move with an equal number of buyers and sellers in it, you can be sure that some form of redistribution is going on.

Mind you, the trend might continue or reverse. Either way, it doesn't matter. What matters is that you know the trend is weak and that now is probably not the time to be banking on trend strategies.

Starting from the left, we can see that there is close to no counter trend bars, bearish in this case, and the bulls make easy progress. Note the angle with which the bulls proceed upwards.

Then comes the first major correction and the counter-trend players push back against the last third of the bull move. Notice how strong the bearish bars are and note their character compared to the bullish bars.

The bulls recover and push the price higher at the original angle and without any bearish presence, which seems odd. This is soon explained as the bears slam price back down and for a while, it looks as if they've managed to form a V top reversal in the trend, which is an extremely rare occurrence.

The price action that follows is a more accurate reflection of the power in the market, with both bulls and bears sharing chunks of the order flow, with overall order flow in the bull's favor but only just. Price here is certainly in an uptrend but looking at the extent of the bearish pushbacks, perhaps we should be on our guard for a bearish reversal. After all order flow is looking pretty sideways at this point.

So how would we approach an options strategy with the chart in the state it is in at the extreme right? Well, for one, any strategy that requires an option beyond the near month is out of the question, given the probability of it turning. Secondly, looking at the order flow, it does seem to be following a channel, doesn't it?

While the channel isn't very clean, if you were aggressive enough, you could consider deploying a collar with the strike prices above and below this channel to take advantage of the price movement. You could also employ some moderately bullish strategies as price approaches the bottom of this channel and figuring out the extent of the bull move is easier thanks to you being able to reference the top of the channel.

As price moves in this channel, it's all well and good. Eventually though, we know that the trend has to flip. How do we know when this happens?

Turning Points

As bulls and bears struggle over who gets to control the order flow, price swings up and down. You will notice that every time price comes back into the 6427-6349 zone, the bulls seem to step in masse and repulse the bears.

This tells us that the bulls are willing to defend this level in large numbers and strongly at that. Given the number of times the bears have tested this level, we can safely assume that above this level, bullish strength is a bit weak. However, at this level, it is as if the bulls have retreated and are treating this as a sort of last resort, for the trend to be maintained. You can see where I'm going with this.

If this level were to be breached by the bears, it is a good bet that a large number of bulls will be taken out. In martial terms, the largest army of bulls has been marshaled at this level. If this force is defeated, it is unlikely that there's going to be too much resistance to the bears below this level.

This zone, in short, is a turning point. If price breaches this zone decisively, we can safely assume that the bears have moved in and control the majority if the order flow.

Turning Point Breached

The decisive turning point zone is marked by the two horizontal lines and the price touches this level twice more and is repulsed by the bulls. Notice how the last bounce before the level breaks produces an extremely weak bullish bounce and price simply caves through this. Notice the strength with which the bears break through.

The FTSE was in a longer uptrend on the weekly chart, so the bulls aren't completely done yet. However, as far as the daily timeframe is concerned, notice how price retests that same level but this time around, it acts as resistance instead of support.

For now, we can conclude that as long as the price remains below the turning point, we are bearishly biased. You can see this by looking at the angle with which bulls push back as well as, the lack of strong bearish participation on the push upwards.

This doesn't mean we go ahead and pencil in a bull move and start implementing strategies that take advantage of the upcoming bullish move. Remember, nothing is for certain in the markets. Don't change your bias or strategy until the turning point decisively breaks.

Some key things to note here are that a turning point is always a major S/R level. It is usually a swing point where a large number of with trend forces gather to support the trend. This will not always be the case, so don't make the mistake of hanging on to older turning points.

The current order flow and price action are what matters the most, so pay attention to that above all else. Also, note how the candles that test this level all have wicks on top of them.

This indicates that the bears are quite strong here and that any subsequent attack will be handled the same way until the level breaks.

Do we know when the level will break? Well, we can't say with any accuracy. However, we can estimate the probability of it breaking.

The latest upswing has seen very little bearish pushback, comparatively speaking, and the push into the level is strong. Instinct would say that there's one more rejection left here. However, who knows? Until the level breaks, we stay bearish. When the level breaks, we switch to the bullish side.

Putting it all Together

So now we're ready to put all of this together into one coherent package. Your analysis should always begin with determining the current state of the market. Ranges are pretty straightforward to spot, and they occur either within big pullbacks in trends or at the end of trends.

CHAPTER 15:

Options Trading Strategies

Options Strategies

We are now going to leave the world of selling options and go back to the one that most people are interested in, which is the world of trading options. We are going to have a look at strategies that can be used to increase the odds of profits when trading options. In reality, some of these strategies involve buying and selling options at the same time. Keep in mind that these techniques will require a higher-level designation from your broker. So, it might not be something you can use right away if you are a beginner.

Strangles

One of the simplest strategies that go beyond simply buying options, hoping to profit on moves of the underlying share price, is called a strangle. This strategy involves buying a call option and a put option simultaneously. They will have the same expiration dates, but different strike prices. If the price of the stock rises the put option will expire worthless (but of course it may still hold a small amount of value when you closed your position, and you can sell it and recoup some of the loss). But you will make a profit off the call option. On the other hand, if the stock price declines, the call option will expire worthlessly, but you can make a profit from the put option.

In this case, you can make substantial profits no matter which way the stock moves, but the larger the move, the more profits. On the upside, the profit potential is theoretically unlimited. On the downside, the stock could theoretically fall to zero, so there is a limit, but potential gains are substantial.

The breakeven price on the upside is the strike price of the call plus the amount of the two premiums settled for the options.

If the stock price declines the breakeven price would be the difference between the strike value of the put option and the sum of the two premiums paid for the options.

Straddles

When you purchase a call and a put option with similar strike amounts and expiration dates, this is called a straddle. The idea here is that the trader is hoping the share price will either rise or fall by a significant amount. It won't matter which way the price moves. Again, if the price rises the put option will expire worthless, if the price falls the call option will expire worthlessly. For example, suppose a stock is trading at $100 a share. We can buy at the money call and put options that expire in 30 days. The price of the call and put options would be $344 and $342 respectively, for a total investment of $686.

With 20 days left to expiration, suppose the share price rises to $107. Then the call is priced at $766, and the put is at $65. We can sell them both at this time, for $831 and make a profit of $145.

Suppose that, instead of at 20 days to expiration, the share price dropped to $92. In that case, the call is priced at $39, and the put is priced at $837. We can sell them for $876, making a profit of $190.

So, although the profits are modest compared to a situation where we had speculated correctly on the directional move of the stock and bought only calls or puts, this way we profit no matter which way the share price moves. The downside to this strategy is that the share price may not move in a big enough way to make profits possible. Remember that extrinsic value will be declining for both the call and the put options.

Selling covered calls against LEAPS and other LEAPS Strategies

A LEAP is a long-term option that is an option that expires at a date that is two years in the future. They are regular options otherwise, but you can do some interesting things with LEAPS. Because the expiration date is so far away, they cost a lot more. Looking at Apple, call options with a $195 strike price that expires in two years are selling for $28.28 (for a total price of $2,828). While that seems expensive, consider that 100 shares of Apple would cost $19,422 at the time of writing.

If you buy in the money LEAPS, then you can use them to sell covered calls. This is an interesting strategy that lets you earn premium income without having actually to buy the shares of stock.

LEAPS can also be used for other investing strategies. For example, if Apple is trading at $194, we can buy a LEAP option for $3,479 with a strike price of $190 that expires in two years. If, at some point during that two-year period, the share price rose to $200 we could exercise the option and buy the shares at $190, saving $10 a share. Also, at the same time, we could have been selling covered calls against the LEAPS.

Buying Put Options as Insurance

A put option gives you the right to sell shares of stock at a certain price. Suppose that you wanted to ensure your investment in Apple stock, and you had purchased 100 shares at $191 a share, for a total investment of $19,000. You are worried that the share price is going to drop and so you could buy a put option as a kind of insurance. Looking ahead, you see a put option with a $190 strike price for $4.10. So, you spend $410 and buy the put option.

Should the price of Apple shares suddenly tumble you could exercise your right under the put option to dispose of your shares by selling at the strike price to minimize your losses. Suppose you wake up one morning and the share price has dropped to $170 for some reason. Had you not bought the option you could have tried to get rid of your shares now and take a loss of $21 a share. But, since you bought the put option, you can sell your shares for $190 a share. That is a $1 loss since you purchased the shares at $191. However, you also have to take into account the premium paid for the put options contract, which was $4.10. So, your total loss would be $5.10 a share, but that is still less than the loss of $21 a share that you would have suffered selling the shares on the market at the $170 price. When investors buy stock and a put at the same time, it is called a married put.

Spreads

Spreads involve buying and selling options simultaneously. This is a more complicated options strategy that is only used by advanced traders. You will have to get a high-level designation with your brokerage in order to use this type of strategy. We won't go into details because these methods are beyond the scope of junior options traders, but we will briefly mention some of the more popular methods so that you can have some awareness.

One of the interesting things about spreads is they can be used by level 3 traders to earn a regular income from options. If you think the price of a stock is going to stay the same or rise, you sell a put credit spread. You sell a higher-priced option and buy a lower-priced option at the same time. The difference in option prices is your profit. There is a chance of loss if the price drops to the strike price of the puts (and you could get assigned if it goes below the strike price of the put option you sold). You can buy back the spread, in that case, to avoid getting assigned.

If you think that the price of a stock is going to drop you can sell to open a credit spread. In this case, you are hoping the price of the stock is going to stay the same or drop. You sell a call with a low strike price and buy a call with a high strike price (both out of the money). The difference in price is your profit, and losses are capped.

We can also consider more complicated spreads.

For example, you can use a diagonal spread with calls. This means you buy a call that has a shorter expiration date but a strike amount that is higher, and then you sell a call with a longer expiration date and a lower strike price. This is done in such a way that you earn more, from selling the call, than you spend on buying the call for a considerable strike amount, and so you get a net credit to your account.

Spreads can become quite complicated, and there are many different types of spreads. If a trader thinks that the price of a stock will only go up a small amount, they can do a bull call spread. Profit and loss are capped in this case. The two options would have the same expiration date.

If you sell a call with a lower strike price and simultaneously buy a call with a high strike price, this is called a bear call spread. You seek to profit if the underlying stock drops in price. This can also be done by using two put options. In that case, you buy a put option that has a higher strike and sell a put option with a lower strike price.

A bull spread involves attempting to profit when the price of the stock rises by a small amount. In this case, you can also use either two call options or two put options. You buy an option with a lower strike price while selling an option with a higher strike price.

Spreads can be combined in more complicated ways. An iron butterfly combines a bear call spread with a bear put spread. The purpose of doing this is to generate steady income while minimizing the risk of loss.

An iron condor uses a put spread, and a call spread together. There would be four options simultaneously, with the same expiration dates but different strike prices. It involves selling both sides (calls and puts).

CHAPTER 16:

Application on the Futures Market

W hat actually happens when you buy futures? – is actually one of the most frequent questions in relation to futures trading. The answer to this question can be summarized in a sentence that states: when you buy futures, you are actually accepting to buy products or services that the company from which you bought futures has not produced yet.

In comparison to stock trading, futures trading is much riskier because you deal with products and services that are not yet produced. With such characteristics, future trading is very popular not only among the producing companies and individuals and customers but also among speculators as well.

While stocks or shares are being traded on stock markets, futures are being traded on futures markets. The idea of future markets developed from the needs of agricultural producers in the mid-nineteenth century where often happened that the demand was much bigger than supply.

The difference between the futures markets and futures markets today is that today's futures markets have crossed the borders of agricultural production and entered many other sectors such as financial. As such, future markets today are used for buying and selling currencies as well as some other financial instruments. What future markets made possible is the opportunity for a farmer to be able to participate in the goods with customers on the other end of the world. One of the biggest and most important future markets is the International Monetary Market (IMM) that was established in 1972.

Futures are financial derivatives that obtain their value from the movement in the price of another asset. It means that the price of futures is not dependent on its inherent value, but on the price of the asset, the futures contract is tracking.

One of the advantages of the futures market is that is centralized and that people from around the world electronically are able to make future contracts. These futures contracts will specify the price of the merchandise and the time of delivery. Besides that, every future contract contains information about the quality and the quantity of the sold goods, specific price and the method in which the goods are to be delivered to the buyers.

A person who buys or sells a futures contract does not pay for the whole value of the contract. He pays a small upfront fee to trigger an open position. For example, if the value of the futures contract is $350,000 when the S&P 500 is 1400, he only pays $21,875 as its initial margin. The exchange sets this margin and may change anytime.

If the S&P 500 moved up to 1500, the futures contract will be worth $375,000. Thus, the person will earn $25,000 in profit. However, if the index fell to 1390 from its original 1400, he will lose $2,500 because the futures contract will now be worth $347,500. This $2,500 is not a realized loss yet. The broker will also not require the individual to add more cash to his trading account.

However, if the index fell to 1300, the futures contract will be worth $325,000. The individual loses $50,000. The broker will require him to add more money to his trading account because his initial margin of $21,875 is no longer enough to cover his losses.

Futures Market Categories

There are similarities in all futures contracts. However, each contract may track different assets. As such, it is important to study the various markets that exist.

You can trade futures contracts on different categories and assets. However, if you are still a new trader, it is important to trade assets that you know. For example, if you are into stock trading for a few years already, you must start with futures contracts using stock indexes. This way, you won't have a hard time understanding the underlying asset. You only need to understand how the futures market works.

After choosing a category, decide on the asset that you want to trade. For example, you want to trade futures contracts in the energy category. Focus on coal, natural gas, crude oil or heating oil. The markets trade at various levels, so you must understand relevant things, like the nuances, liquidity, margin requirements, contract sizes and volatility. Do the necessary research before trading in futures contracts.

Types of Trade

A basis trade allows you to go long or short on a futures contract and go short or long on the cash market. It is a wager that the difference in price between the two markets will fluctuate. For example, you decide to buy a 10-year US Treasury bond futures then sell a physical 10-year US Treasury bond.

A spread trade allows you to go short and long on two futures contracts. It is a wager that the difference in price between the futures contracts will change. For example, you buy an S&P 500 futures contract for August delivery and sell an S&P 500 futures contract for November delivery.

A hedging trade allows you to sell a futures contract to offset a position you hold in the current market. For example, a stock trader does not want to sell his shares for tax reasons. However, he is fearful of a sharp decline in the stock market so he sells S&P 500 futures contract as a hedge.

An important issue that must be mention in regards to futures and futures contracts is the notion of prices and the limits of future contracts. In future contracts, prices are expressed in classical currencies such as US dollars. The prices in the aspect of future contracts also have the minimum amount of money for which the price of the product may go up or go down. This minimum in the context of futures contracts is referred to as "ticks".

These tricks are very important for an investor who is investing huge sums of money or is buying a huge number of products because the fluctuation of prices can have enormous influence on the amount of money spent on certain products. It must also be noted that these "ticks" are not the same for each merchandise. Every commodity in the trading of futures has its own "ticks", the minimum for price fluctuation and it depends on the type of commodity.

How Can We Make a Profit on the Futures Markets?

One thing to remember, is, that even if you buy and sell futures contracts in commodities, you don't actually take delivery of the underlying commodity. You would close out your contracts before the delivery date.

Let's take a simple example and relate that to a futures contract. You saw a house for sale for $300 000. You believe that in the next year its value will appreciate by about 10% but the downside is you don't have enough money to buy the house outright so you decide to put down a deposit of $30 000. One year later the property has appreciated in value, as expected, by 10% and is now worth $330 000. You decide to sell the property and make a profit of $30 000. Your initial investment was $30 000 and you sold the house at a profit of $30 000, which gives you a 100% profit on your investment.

Commodity trading works very similarly. Let's take an example. You've been analyzing the corn market and you expect the prices to increase, so you decide to buy the September contract which is presently trading at $2.40 per bushel. There are 5000 bushels in a corn contract. You pay a $500 deposit or margin as required by the exchange.

After four weeks the price has increased to $3.40 a bushel, as expected. This means the contract value is now $3.40 X 5000 = $17000. You bought the contract at $12000 ($2.40 X 5000) four weeks ago and you made a profit of $5000 ($17000 -$14000). The return on your investment of $500 is 1000% in just 4 weeks.

You can also make profits when market prices drop. Let's say you anticipate a drop in the soybeans price from its current level of $5.00 per bushel. There are also 5000 bushels in a soybean contract. You decide to sell one September contract at the current level. You pay a $1000 deposit or margin. Six weeks later the price has dropped considerably, as expected, to $3.50 per bushel. You decide to close your position and take your profits. You do this by buying a contract to offset the contract you sold six weeks earlier. The difference between the price you sold and the price bought back is your profit. $25000($5.00 X 5000) − $17500($3.5 X 5000) = $7500 profit for an investment of $1000. 750% profit in six weeks.

Selling Short - How does it work?

How can one make money when the market is dropping? This is something that happens around us every day of our lives. Let's say you are a car dealer and you sell brand new cars. The factory-supplied you with a couple of cars on consignment that you can display on your showroom floor and you don't have to pay for them right away because the factory allows you some time to sell them. After a while, you sell one of the cars for $50 000 and now you have to pay the factory, but only $30 000, which is the cost price to you that leaves you with a profit of

$20 000. What did you actually do? You borrowed the car from the factory and sold it to your client at a higher price than the factory charges you and that way you made money. You sold first and bought it later. When we sell futures we do the same thing, we sell high because we anticipate the market will trade down and we can buy back or close our position at a lower price and make a profit. Just like the car dealer.

There Must Be Risks?

With any business you have risks. When you open a business you have to invest huge amounts of capital upfront to set up your business. You have to rent offices, buy stock and pay salaries, etc. before the first customer walks through your door. You have no idea how many customers will walk in or whether you will generate enough business to even recover your capital expenses. With the speculative markets it's the same but how you manage your risk will determine your success.

Let's compare the stock market with the futures market, you can diversify your risk in the stock market by investing in different non-correlated stock and under normal circumstances it will work well but sudden political changes or news regarding the economy can affect all share prices overnight, even if you did spread your investments across a number of companies, all your profits can be wiped in extreme situations, as we have seen in recent years.

Comparing this to futures markets where you can spread your investments across a diverse range of commodity markets like corn, silver, oil, sugar, wheat or cotton, it's impossible to imagine any situation affecting all these markets at the same time. Economic disasters, droughts, war, floods, and political events will always happen and they also affect certain commodity markets, but spreading your investment not only minimizes your losses but also puts you in a position to benefit from any price move.

CHAPTER 17:

Which Market to Trade and with which Broker

Thre is a huge array of products to trade with on offer but for scalping you need products with large volumes exchanged and volatility. I find these in the mini DAX and the e-mini Dow futures. The volatility, i.e. daily range (distance between the low of the day and the high of the day) is wide. In addition, and this point is very important, these products are traded on regulated and centralized markets: Eurex for the DAX futures and CME for the e-mini Dow; as opposed to CFDs which are OTC products; i.e. your broker is the counterpart of your trade. When you buy, your broker is your seller and when you sell, your broker is buying from you. On the other hand, on a centralized market, your order is routed and executed when someone else's order matches yours (buyers' and sellers' prices meet). In addition, on the future markets you can see the volume of transactions, while on the CFD, your broker may show no volume at all or only the volumes exchanged on their platform.

And more importantly, in the future markets you see the prices offered by other market participants while on CFDs, you only get the prices offered by your broker. To illustrate, this I have just taken below a snapshot of prices offered by two different CFD brokers at the same time.

Ticket order

Which broker offers the right price?

In case of high volatility, CFDs do not react the same way as futures: the prices may adjust at a different pace and the spread offered by the broker may increase. A market order may even be repriced if the market is moving very quickly. Stop orders may incur slippage which means you will lose few points to your broker as the price you are paid is few points away from your stop order.

I like to compare CFDs and futures to the current trends in grocery consumption. People like to consume fresh products that come directly from the farm, without any middlemen and wholesalers that make their margin in the process. Well, trading futures is similar. You get the prices directly from the market while CFDs are products offered by your broker who gets their revenue through the spreads. Moreover, CFD providers hedge their positions or some part of them using futures and options.

So, I can only recommend that you trade with future or mini future contracts. However, CFDs can be useful to trade small positions when you make your first steps in trading as you can trade products at only one euro per point instead of 5 euros on a mini future contract or even 25 euros per points on the DAX future. Note that CFDs are not available in all countries due to local laws and financial regulation.

But if you can and want to trade CFDs, make sure you look at the spreads offered by different brokers before choosing who to trade with. Half a point is not much difference, but in scalping it means a lot. After 20 trades, paying half a point more on each trade at one euro per point will result in an extra 10 euros wasted in commissions; and so on, after 40 trades, you will have wasted 20 euros. Let's say in a month if you perform 600 to 800 trades, you will then have wasted 300 to 400 euros in extra commissions.

How to choose your broker:

In order to be able to scalp in good conditions, you need to look out for the following points when choosing your broker:

- Tight spreads if you choose to work with CFDs. One euro or dollar per point is the maximum you should pay as you don't want to be working just for your broker;

- Real time data flux is essential. The subscription to the Eurex data flux (DAX and mini DAX) will cost you about 20 euros per month and another 25 euros for a subscription to CME CBOT (e-mini Dow) data. Your broker collects the fees for the data supplier; you don't need to pay the supplier directly. If you just want to trade CFDs you won't have to pay these fees, but you will have only access to the data provided by your broker.

- Most of the platforms will let you place simple orders such as buy limit or sell limit orders, with the option to set up an automated take profit and stop loss orders. But some go even further by letting you set up an automated order for part of the position and another one for the second part of the position and so on if you want to set up 3 different targets. I

- Be aware that some brokers operate with a first in first out rule which means that they won't let you have opposite positions on the same product run separately, a.k.a. hedging. A new executed sell order may not open a position but offset or close an already opened buy position. On the other hand, CFD brokers may let you trade, hedge and operate your positions separately from one another. While short and long positions of equivalent quantities and on the same product offset each other in theory, your broker may still calculate a margin cover for each position separately. So, keep an eye on your margin usage.

- If you are starting with a small account, i.e. with less than € 5,000 look for brokers that will let you trade on small quantities, as small as 1/100th of one lot. That way you can start trading taking minimum risk until you build confidence in your trading.

- Being able to trade from a smartphone, an iPad or similar. I certainly cannot recommend that you use these devices for your scalping, but they shall be used as part of plan B if a problem comes up with your computer while you are trading or if your internet broadband suddenly shuts down or resets itself. Your smartphone connected to a mobile phone network will be your back up device to modify or close some orders if necessary, until your computer and the internet are back up and running. Most brokers offer mobile technology in today's world.

- This was the plan B. The plan C is that you should be able to call your broker's trading desk as a last resort, in case of emergency, if your computer and your mobile application don't let you perform an action that needs to be done.

- Lastly, you absolutely need to work with a minimum of two brokers because if for any reason there is a technical problem on one of your brokers' platforms, you need to able to act swiftly on your second broker's platform. Let's say you need to close a position but broker A's platform for some reason is not working. Then you can always open an opposite order on broker's B platform. For instance, you need to close a long position with broker A, but a technical problem doesn't let you do so. Then you should open a short position with broker B, until everything is back up and running. Then you can work on closing these positions simultaneously afterwards.

Once you are ready to trade with the mini futures, I recommend that you have at least 12,000 euros to be able to scalp with 2 lots when the occasion occurs. For the most accurate information, choose the tick by tick data flux if you can choose a data provider. Some data providers offer market data sent to your computer on a second by second basis while others have their data refreshed on a tick by tick basis, which is every time a transaction occurs on the market, showing you the latest price exchanged.

You may want to explore and trade some additional markets, but I recommend not trading more than two markets at a time because scalping requires concentration and prompt action in your trades.

CHAPTER 18:

Application on the Stocks Market

A stock is a form of security that suggests proportional ownership in a company. Stocks are acquired and sold predominantly on stock exchanges, however, there can be private arrangements as well. These exchanges/trades need to fit within government laws which are expected to shield investors from misleading practices. Stocks can be obtained from a large number of online platforms.

Businesses issue (offer) stock to raise capital. The holder of stock (a shareholder) has now acquired a portion of the company and share its profit and loss. Therefore, a shareholder is considered an owner of the company. Ownership is constrained by the amount of shares an individual owns in regard to the amount of shares the company is divided into. For example, if a company has 1,000 shares of stock and one individual owns 100 shares, that individual would receive 10% of the company's capital and profits.

Financial experts don't own companies as such; instead, they sell shares offered by companies. Under the law, there are different types of companies and some are viewed as independent because of how they have set up their businesses. Regardless of the type of company, ultimately, they must report costs, income, changes in structure, etc., or they can be sued. A business set up as an "independent," known as a sole proprietorship, suggests that the owner assumes all responsibilities and is liable for all financial aspects of the business. A business set up as a company of any sort means that the business is separate from its owners and the owners aren't personally responsible for the financial aspects of the business.

This separation is of extreme importance; it limits the commitment of both the company and the shareholder/owner. If the business comes up short, a judge may rule for the company to be liquidated – however, your very own assets will not come under threat. The court can't demand that you sell your shares, though the value of your shares will have fallen significantly.

Trading is the basic idea of exchanging one thing for another. In this regard it is buying or selling, where compensation is paid by a buyer to a seller. Trade can happen inside an economy among sellers and buyers. Overall, trade allows countries to develop markets for the exchange of goods and services that for the most part wouldn't have been available otherwise. It is the reason why an American purchaser can choose between a Japanese, German, or American conduit. Due to overall trade, the market contains progressively significant competition which makes it possible for buyers to get products and services at affordable costs.

In fiscal markets, trading implies the buying and selling of insurances, for instance, the purchase of stock on the New York Stock Exchange (NYSE).

Fundamentals of stock/securities exchange

The exchange of stocks and securities happen on platforms like the New York Stock Exchange and Nasdaq. Stocks are recorded on a specific exchange, which links buyers and sellers, allowing them to trade those stocks. The trade is tracked in the market and allows buyers to get company stocks at fair prices. The value of these stocks move – up or down – depending on many factors in the market. Investors are able to look at these factors and make a decision on whether or not they want to purchase these stocks.

A market record tracks the value of a stock, which either addresses the market with everything taken into account or a specific fragments of the market. You're likely going to hear most about the S&P 500, the Nasdaq composite and the Dow Jones Industrial Average in this regard.

Financial advisors use data to benchmark the value of their own portfolios and, some of the time, to shed light on their stock exchanging decisions. You can also put your assets into an entire portfolio based on the data available in the market.

Stock exchanging information

Most financial experts would be well-taught to build a portfolio with a variety of different financial assets. However, experts who prefer a greater degree of movement take more interest in stock exchanging. This type of investment incorporates the buying and selling of stocks.

The goal of people who trade in stock is to use market data and things happening in the market to either sell stock for a profit, or buy stocks at low prices to make a profit later. Some stock traders are occasional investors, which means they buy and sell every now and then. Others are serious investors, making as little as twelve exchanges for every month.

Financial experts who exchange stocks do wide research, as often as possible, devoting hours day by day tracking the market. They rely upon particular audits, using instruments to chart a stock's advancements attempting to find trading openings and examples. Various online middlemen offer stock exchanging information, including expert reports, stock research, and charting tools.

What is a bear market?

A bear market means stock prices are falling — limits move to 20% or more — based on data referenced previously.

Progressive financial experts may be alright with the term bear market. Profiting in the trade business will always far outlasts the typical bear market; which is why in a bear market, smart investors will hold their shares until the market recovers. This has been seen time and time again. The S&P 500, which holds around 500 of the greatest stocks in the U.S., has consistently maintained an average of around 7% consistently, when you factor in reinvested profits and varied growth. That suggests that if you invested $1,000 30 years ago, you could have around $7,600 today.

Stock market crash versus correction

A crash happens when the commercial value prices fall by 10% or more. It is an unexpected, incredibly sharp fall in stock prices; for example, in October 1987, when stocks dove 23% in a single day.

The stock market tends to be affected longer by crashes in the market and can last from two to nine years.

The criticalness of improvement

You can't avoid the possibility of bear markets or the economy crashing, or even losing money while trading. What you can do, however, is limit the effects these types of market will have on your investment by maintaining a diversified portfolio.

Diversification shields your portfolio from unavoidable market risks. If you dump a large portion of your cash into one means of investment, you're betting on growth that can rapidly turn to loss by a large number of factors. To cushion risks, financial specialists expand by pooling different types of stocks together, offsetting the inevitable possibility that one stock will crash and your entire portfolio will be affected or you lose everything.

You can put together individual stocks and assets in a single portfolio. One recommendation: dedicate 10% or less of your portfolio to a few stocks you believe in each time you decide to invest.

Ways to invest

There are different ways for new investors to purchase stocks. If you need to pay very low fees, you will need to invest additional time making your own trades. If you wish to beat the market, however, you'll pay higher charges by getting someone to trade on your behalf. If you don't have the time or interest, you may need to make do with lower results. Most stock purchasers get anxious when the market is doing well. Incredibly, this makes them purchase stocks when they are the most volatile. Obviously, business share that is not performing well triggers fear. That makes most investors sell when the costs are low. Choosing what amount to invest is an individual decision. It depends upon your comfort with risk. It depends upon your ability and capacity to invest energy into getting some answers concerning the stock exchange.

Purchase Stocks Online

Purchasing stocks online costs the least, yet gives little encouragement. You are charged a set price, or a percent of your purchase, for every trade. It very well may be the least secure. It expects you to teach yourself altogether on the best way to invest. Consequently, it additionally takes the most time. It's a smart idea to check the top web based trading sites before you begin.

Investment Groups

Joining an investment group gives you more data at a sensible price. However, it takes a great deal of effort to meet with the other group members. They all have different degrees of expertise. You might be required to pool a portion of your assets into a group account before trading. Once more, it's a smart idea to examine the better investment groups before you begin.

Full-time Brokers

A full-time broker is costly on the grounds that you'll pay higher fees. Nevertheless, you get more data and assistance and that shields you from greed and fear. You should search around to choose a decent broker that you can trust. The Securities and Trade Commission shares helpful tips on the best ways to choose a broker.

Money Manager

Money managers select and purchase the stocks for you. You pay them a weighty charge, typically 1-2 percent of your complete portfolio. If the chief progresses admirably, it takes minimal amount of time. That is on the grounds that you can simply meet with them more than once per year. Ensure you realize how to choose a decent financial advisor.

File Fund

Otherwise called market traded assets, record assets can be a cheap and safe approach to benefit from stocks. They essentially track the stocks in a file. Models incorporate the MSCI developing business sector record. The reserve rises and falls alongside the file. There is no yearly cost. However, it's difficult to outflank the market along these lines since record supports just track the market. All things being equal, there are a great deal of valid justifications why you ought to put resources into a file funds.

Common Funds

Common assets are a generally more secure approach to benefit from stocks. The company supervisor will purchase a gathering of stocks for you. You don't possess the stock, yet a portion of the investment. Most assets have a yearly cost, between 0.5 percent to 3 percent. They guarantee to outflank the S&P 500, or other equivalent file reserves. For additional information, see 16 Best Tips on Mutual Fund Basics and Before You Buy a Mutual Fund.

Theories of stock investments

Theories of stock investments look like basic resources. Both of them pool all of their investors' dollars into one viably supervised hold. In any case, theories stock investments put assets into ensnared fiscal instruments known as subordinates. They guarantee to win the normal resources with these significantly used theories.

Theoretical stock investments are private companies, not open organizations. That suggests they aren't coordinated by the SEC. They are risky, yet various investors acknowledge this higher danger prompts a better yield.

Selling Your Stocks

As important as buying stocks is knowing when to sell them. Most financial experts buy when the stock exchange is rising and sell when it's falling. Regardless, a clever money marketer seeks after a strategy subject to their financial needs.

You should reliably watch out for the noteworthy market records. The three greatest U.S. records are the Dow Jones Industrial Average, the S&P 500, and the Nasdaq. In any case, don't solidify in case they enter a modification or a mishap. Those events don't prop up long.

CHAPTER 19:

How Does The Stock Market Work?

The stock market is not like your neighborhood grocery store: you can only buy and sell through licensed brokers who make trades on major indexes like NASDAQ and S&P 100. This is where investors meet up to buy and sell stocks or other financial investments like bonds. The stock market is made up of so many exchanges, like the NASDAQ or the New York Exchange. These exchanges are not open all through the day. Most exchanges like the NASDAQ and NYSE are open from 9:30 am to 4 pm. EST. Although premarket and trading after closing time now exist, not all brokers do this.

Companies list their stocks on an exchange in a bid to raise money for their business, and investors buy those shares. In addition to this, investors can trade shares among themselves, and the exchange keeps track of the rate of supply and demand of each listed stock. The rate of supply and demand for stocks determines the price. If there's a high demand for a particular stock, its price tends to rise. On the other hand, the price of a stock goes down when there's less demand for it. The stock market computer algorithm handles these varying fluctuations in prices.

How Does The Stock Market Work?

A Stock market analysis definitely looks like gibberish to beginners and average investors. However, you should know that the way this market works is actually quite simple. Just imagine a typical auction house or an online auction website. This market works in the same way - it allows buyers and sellers to negotiate prices and carry out successful trades. The first stock market took place in a physical marketplace, however, these days, trades happen electronically via the internet and online stockbrokers. From the comfort of your homes, you can easily bid and negotiate for the prices of stocks with online stockbrokers.

Furthermore, you might come across news headlines that say the stock market has crashed or gone up. Once again, don't fret or get all excited when you come across such news. Most often than not, this means a stock market index has gone up or down. In other words, the stocks in a market index have gone down. Before we proceed, let's explore the meaning of market indexes.

Stock Market Indexes

Market indexes track the performance of a group of stocks in a particular sector like manufacturing or technology. The value of the stocks featured in an index is representative of all the stocks in that sector. It is very important to take note of what stocks each market index represents. In addition to this, giant market indexes like the Dow Jones Industrial Average, the NASDAQ composite, and the Standard & Poor's 500, are often used as proxies for the performance of the stock market as a whole. You can choose to invest in an entire index through the exchange-traded funds and index funds, as it can track a specific sector or index of the stock market.

Bullish and Bearish Markets

Talking about the bullish outlook of the stock market is guaranteed to get beginners looking astonished. Yes, it sounds ridiculous at first, but with time, you get to appreciate the ingenuity of these descriptions. Let's start with the bearish market. A bear is an animal you would never want to meet on a hike; it strikes fear into your heart, and that's the effect you will get from a bearish market. The threshold for a bearish market varies within a 20 percent loss or more.

Most young investors unfamiliar with a bear market as we've been in a bull market since the first quarter of 2019. In fact, this makes it the second-longest bull market in history. Just as you have probably guessed by now, a bull market indicates that stock prices are rising. You should know that the market is continually changing from bull to bear and vice versa. From the Great Recession to the global market crash, these changing market prices indicate the start of larger economic patterns. For instance, a bull market shows that investors are investing heavily and that the economy is doing extremely well. On the other hand, a bear market shows investors are scared and pulling back, with the economy on the brink of collapsing. If this made you paranoid about the next bear market, don't fret. Business analysts have shown that the average bull market generally outlasts the average bear market by a large margin.

This is why you can grow your money in stocks over an extended period of time.

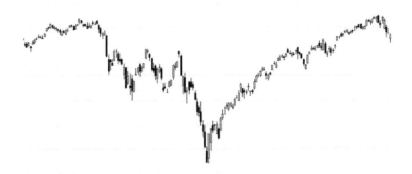

Stock Market Corrections and Crash

A stock market crash is every investor's nightmare. It is usually extremely difficult to watch stocks that you've spent so many years accumulating diminish before your very eyes. Yes, this is how volatile the stock market is. Stock market crashes usually include a very sudden and sharp drop in stock prices, and it might herald the beginning of a bear market. On the other hand, stock market corrections occur when the market drops by 10 percent - this is just the market's way of balancing itself. The current bull market has gone through 5 market corrections.

Analyzing the Stock Market

You are not psychic. It is nearly impossible to accurately predict the outcome of your stock to the last detail. However, you can become near perfect at reading the stock market by learning how to properly analyze the components of this market. There are two basic types of analyses: technical analysis and fundamental analysis.

Fundamental Market Analysis

Fundamental analysis involves getting data about a company's stocks or a particular sector in the stock market, via financial records, company assets, economic reports, and market share. Analysts and investors can conduct fundamental analysis via the metrics on a corporation's financial statement. These metrics include cash flow statements, balance sheet statements, footnotes, and income statements. Most times, you can get a company's financial statement through a 10-k report in the database. In addition to this, the SEC's EDGAR is a good place to get the financial statement of the company you are interested in. With the financial statement, you can deduce the revenues, expenses, and profits a company has made.

What's more? By looking at the financial statement, you will have a measure of a company's growth trajectory, leverage, liquidity, and solvency. Analysts utilize different ratios to make an accurate prediction about stocks. For example, the quick ratio and current ratio are useful in determining if a company will be able to pay its short-term liabilities with the current asset. If the current ratio is less than 1, the company is in poor financial health and may not be able to recover from its short-term debt. Here's another example: a stock analyst can use the debt ratio to measure the current level of debt taken on by the company. If the debt ratio is above 1, it means the company has more debt than assets and it's only a matter of time before it goes under.

Technical Market Analysis

This is the second part of stock market analysis and it revolves around studying past market actions to predict the stock price direction. Technical analysts put more focus on the price and volume of shares. Additionally, they analyze the market as a whole and study the supply and demand factors that dictate market movement. In technical analyses, charts are of inestimable value. Charts are a vital tool as they show the graphical representation of a stock's trend within a set time frame. What's more? Technical investors are able to identify and mark certain areas as resistance or support levels on a chart. The resistance level is a previous high stock price before the current price. On the other hand, support levels are represented by a previous low before the current stock price. Therefore, a break below the support levels marks the beginning of a bearish trend. Alternatively, a break above the resistance level marks the beginning of a bullish market trend. Technical analysis is only effective when the rise and fall of stock prices are influenced by supply and demand forces. However, technical analysis is mostly rendered ineffective in the face of outside forces that affect stock prices such as stock splits, dividend announcements, scandals, changes in management, mergers, and so on. Investors can make use of both types of analyses to get an accurate prediction of their stock values.

Why You Need To Diversify

According to research by Ned Davis, a bear market occurs every 3.5 years and has an average lifespan of 15 months. One thing is clear, though: you can't avoid bear markets. You can, however, avoid the risks that come with investing in a single investment portfolio. Let's look at a common mistake that new investors typically make. Research points to the fact that individual stocks dwindle to a loss of 100 percent. By throwing in your lot with one company, you are exposing yourself to many setbacks. For example, you can lose your money if a corporation is embroiled in a scandal, poor leadership, and regulatory issues. So, how can you balance out your losses? By investing in therefore mentioned index fund or ETF fund, as these indexes hold many different stocks, as by doing this, you've automatically diversified your investment. Here's a nugget to cherish: put 90 percent of your investment funds in an index fund, and put the remaining 10 percent in an individual stock that you trust.

When to Sell Your Stocks

One thing is sure - you are not going to hold your stocks forever. All our investment advice and energies are directed towards buying. Yes, it is the buying of stocks that kick-start the whole investment when chasing your dream concept. However, just as every beginning has an end, you will eventually sell every stock you buy. It is the natural order. Even so, selling off stock is not an easy decision. Heck! It's even harder to determine the right time to sell. This is the point where greed and human emotions start to battle with pragmatism. Many investors try to make sensible selling decisions solely based on price movements. However, this is not a sure strategy, as it is still sensible to hold onto a stock that has fallen in value. Conversely, selling a stock when it has reached your target is seen as prudent. So, how can you navigate around this dilemma?

Why Selling Is So Hard

Do you know why it's so hard to let go of your stocks even when you have a fixed strategy to follow? The answer lies in human greed. When making decisions, it's an innate human tendency to be greedy.

CHAPTER 20:

Application on the Forex Market

Trading Platforms

If there's something essentially needed to trade Forex, it is a trading platform! If you are assuming that trading is ideal for absolute beginners, I'd say yes, but you are not going to make millions overnight. If you look at Forex trading like gambling, you will not be able to become a profitable trader because greed will invade you. If you want to become a great trader, you must have skills and patience. Also, you must keep practicing trading as it helps to shape up your trading style into a better version. Once you do your homework, you'd feel as if you are good to go. But then, Forex trading knowledge can't be accumulated into a few pages or days. It is a continuous learning process. If you have just started with the basics of Forex trading, you have a lot more to learn. A beginner should have access to a user-friendly platform that can be easily handled when trading.

A beginner's journey is already complex, so when the trader doesn't select the right platform, the difficulties increase. When the trading platform is easy to understand, you will not have difficulties when trying out new strategies and techniques on the demo account. There are many reliable brokers that you can select when you are trading Forex, but the problem is finding the ideal broker. To earn extra income, Forex is a good choice. But it doesn't mean Forex can be traded as the main source of income. However, either main income or part-time income, you must find the ideal broker and an excellent platform to keep going in trading. Even though there are many good brokers, you must do your research to find the right one that offers the most straightforward trading platform. I know, you will encounter difficulties when selecting the right broker, so let me help you.

Before you settle for an ideal platform check whether the platform is reliable; it is one of the most crucial factors that you must consider when selecting a trading platform. You don't want to lose all the money that you collected, so make sure to find a platform that you can rely on. If you're going to deposit and withdraw your cash without facing any issues, the trading platform must be reliable.

Another important factor is charges related to the platform. You must consider the charges because your profits will disappear even before you know it if the charges are high. Besides, you are just starting your journey so your income will not be massive. The smaller income that you gain must be protected, so for that, you must consider the charges related to the trading platform.

You must next consider the licensing factor of the Forex platforms. If the relevant authorities monitor the platform, they are unlikely to fool you. The trading platforms will work according to terms and conditions, so you don't have to worry when you are trading through it. But to find whether the platform is licensed, you must do some research even if it is tough. Along with these, you must consider the simplicity in the Forex trading platform, but due to the software used, eventually, almost all the trading platforms have become easier to handle. In the meantime, don't forget to consider the leverage, margin, and other requirements that generally should be considered when selecting a trading platform. Once you select the ideal platform, you will be able to trade in a hassle-free way. However, there's more to learn about Forex trading platforms. So, keep reading!

There are two types of platforms, such as commercial and prop platforms. Before you pick any, you must ensure to understand the types in detail. Thus, prop platforms are designed by Forex brokers, and specialized companies develop commercial platforms. However, there are unique features for both the trading platforms. Even though the prop platforms are considerable, there are times when you might want to change the broker. But when you try to do it, you have to learn the new platform from scratch.

Basically, prop platforms are not suitable for naïve traders because you might have to struggle a lot to understand the sophisticated features. But, why do these trading platforms include complex features? Well, a Forex broker's main duty is not to create and manage trading platforms. Hence, they don't spend much time to introduce better trading tools and features to prop platforms. For example, if you consider Aplari or FXCM you might find it difficult to handle because brokers develop these. Beginners like you need a lot of time to get adjusted with the trading platform. But, I don't say trade execution speed is terrible because it is excellent in prop platforms, yet beginners will have a tough time understanding this platform.

So, beginners like you can consider the platforms designed by professional companies. One of the most common trading software is Metatrader. This is a user-friendly and high standard platform that you can consider even if you don't have experience. But if you are looking for a platform that includes broker feeds, then this is not going to help because the commercial platform has poor customization. These companies sell commercial platforms to Forex brokers so the benefits may be biased towards the broker, but not the trader. Yet, as beginners, you are not going to find anything better than commercial platforms because they are extremely user-friendly and flexible.

So that's about the types of platforms that you will come across. But, I'm pretty sure you'll have some doubts related to selecting the right trading platform. Hence, I'll solve some of the common questions below.

What to consider when selecting the right platform?

You already know this, yet let me provide a brief answer. But, before you make a decision, it is better to read some reviews about the platform so that you will make a solid decision.

Which Forex software will be ideal?

A technical trader must consider a comfortable charting platform. The platform that you have selected must have all the necessary tools. Only if you select the right trading platform will you be able to enjoy trading.

A fundamental trader must consider the news and analysis factor and check whether it is accessible by the Forex software that the trader has selected.

Should you trust the platforms that provide exclusive offers?

You already know when something is too good to be true, we shouldn't rely on it. Just like that, if a platform is providing exclusive things that you cannot fathom, then you must think twice before considering that platform. If they are offering so much, they should have massive profits. If yes, then from where do they get so much profit? Instead of falling for exclusive offers, you can find a platform that is reliable and reasonable.

I hope these questions and answers cleared most doubts that you had about trading platforms. However, it is better to get some idea about the famous trading platforms. Let's get started!

MetaTrader 5

Both MT4 and MT5 were introduced by one company some time back. The best thing about MetaTrader 5 is that you can use it to trade options and stock trading. Most traders who trade on the stock market along with the Forex market consider MT5 because it is simple and beneficial.

MetaTrader 4

Currently, a higher percentage of traders use MetaTrader 4 to trade Forex. Even brokers recommend MT4 as the best trading platform. Yet, certain fund managers and professional traders don't prefer MT4.

Beginners like you can benefit immensely from this platform because it is user-friendly. If you have selected the right broker who offers MT4, you will be able to enjoy comparatively cheap prices. Also, this is an old platform provided to Forex traders. You must also note that this platform has a great team to solve issues related to trading. But sadly, fund managers believe that trade execution is not as fast as they want.

NinjaTrader

This is the oldest platform remaining in the industry. Even now, some traders prefer using this trading platform because it is easy to handle. Also, this platform has special features that can be enjoyed by traders.

TradeStation

This is for fund managers and professional traders because this platform has speed and high-end technology required by professional traders and managers. This platform has some issues with the user-friendly option, but fund managers and professional traders don't worry about it.

Finally, you must understand that the trading platform is all about how comfortable you are with the platform. It should provide an easy path to enter and exit trades while providing a user-friendly feature. If you select the right platform, you will be able to make a solid trading decision. But, making profits will depend on your skill, so you can't entirely depend on the trading platform. Of course, it is a supporting factor, but it is not a reason to make profits. If you want to reach success in trading, you must not think twice to get help from Forex mentors and professionals. Anyway, let me provide some insights into some other factors as well.

Opening an Account

You must be excited about Forex trading. But, without learning the ways to open an account, how will you even trade? With online Forex trading, the excitement to trade Forex has increased immensely. However, to start trading Forex, you must find a broker, select a trading platform, and then open an account. But the part of opening an account is pretty easy. To open an account, you need certain things including name, email, address, contact number, account type, a password for the account, citizenship, date of birth, employment details, Tax ID, and a few more financial questions. The steps of opening an account will differ from one broker to another, yet the following are the general procedures to open an account:

Sometimes, you might have to fill the application with the details related to the trading experience.

Select the broker and check for the suitable and available account.

After completing the application, register with your username, and then you'll receive the credentials to your Forex trading account. Now, you'll have access to the broker's client portal.

And then, transfer the deposit funds through any of the possible payment methods to your trading account. But remember, you might have to bear charges as per the payment method.

Once the funding procedure is complete, you can then trade Forex. But, your broker will provide necessary guidance and ideas before you enter into live trading.

Once you complete these procedures, you are good to begin your journey. But, are you wondering why you have to follow all these hectic rules and regulations? Well, the Forex market wasn't filled with rules and regulations, but once the market allowed retail trading, the rules and regulations became compulsory. If the market wasn't strict, it would be easy for the market participants to gamble on the market. The factor of reliability will become questionable. Also, you will not find brokers who don't require these details. On the other hand, if you find brokers who don't ask these questions, then you have to think about opening an account.

Well, an important thing about opening an account is risk disclosure. As a beginner, you are likely to be mindless about this factor, but remember, this is very important

CHAPTER 21

Application on the Commodities Market

Trading in the commodity markets based on fundamental news and analysis differs dramatically from the quick-natured technical analysis, which often requires traders to shift from bullish to bearish in the blink of an eye. Fundamental analysis provides slow-handed guidance to traders. In general, the practice of entering or exiting trades based on market fundamentals is a dawdling and tedious process, demanding massively deep pockets and patience. Imagine being a fundamentalist who identified oil as being overvalued near $100 per barrel in 2008, or on the multiple occasion's oil moved above $100 from 2011 to 2013. Initially, a trader selling a futures contract solely on fundamentals would have either blown out his trading account, given up on the trade before it paid off, or suffered a roughly $50,000 drawdown before having an opportunity to profit from the correct analysis. This is because each dollar of crude oil price change equals a profit or loss of $1,000 to a one-lot futures trader. In 2008, the price of oil reached $150 per barrel before suffering from a steep decline. On subsequent occasions, the suffering would have been limited to about $10,000 to $15,000, but still a painful endeavor.

If you are familiar with the popular commodity trading book Hot Commodities, written by Jim Rogers, this slow-paced fundamental approach is exactly what he writes about. Not all of us have the capital to employ such a longterm view in the leveraged world of commodities, as Mr. Rogers does. Accordingly, before assuming commodity trading is as "easy" as that particular book implies, you must consider the vast financial difference in the reality of most commodity traders and the author.

Other than obtaining a big-picture consensus of the market makeup, relying on fundamental analysis alone can be a daunting task for the average trader. After all, it can take months, or even years, for traders to get their hands on absolutely accurate fundamental information. By then, the markets have already moved. Alternatively, during times in which markets are ignoring fundamentals, it can take months, or years, for prices to revert to a more equilibrium price.

What Is Fundamental Analysis?

Fundamental analysis of the commodity markets involves the study of the interaction between supply and demand; with this analysis, traders attempt to predict future price movement. Specifically, the entire concept of fundamental analysis is built upon the following equations:

Demand > Supply = Higher prices

Supply > Demand = Low prices

Most analysts agree that commodity market supply and demand figures are quantifiable, yet even the diehard fundamentalists will admit accurate statistics are not available in real time. Thus, any numbers plugged into the simple and neat formulas given are relatively meaningless. If you input garbage data into the formula, the result will also be garbage. Accordingly, when an analyst runs the numbers she is almost certainly working with either outdated or inaccurate data. Fundamental analysts waiting for confirmed government supply and demand data will be calculating months after the fact. Alternatively, if they are calculating based on estimates (whether they are government or personally derived), it is nothing more than a guess.

Most recall the simple supply and demand cross charts taught in high school and college economic courses; unfortunately, this academic practice erroneously simplifies a concept that is actually highly complex. In my opinion, what appears to be the most straightforward form of commodity market analysis—fundamental—is actually the most difficult in practice.

Because of the massive complexity that comes with estimating current supply and demand details of any given commodity, the seemingly simple mathematical equation fundamentalists use to speculate on prices can be confusing at best, but misleading at worst. In addition, regardless of the time dedicated to deciphering the market's fundamental code, it can be extremely problematic for a trader to succeed using this method of analysis alone.

In order to understand the place of the commodity markets, one needs to consider the bigger picture.

Asset classes are certainly not limited to these five groups, but these are the most common categories. Obviously, any classification is rather arbitrary or, at least, subjective. Even wine or art can be seen as specific asset classes, as much as volatility or weather. On the basis of any assets, including the latter, derivatives or structured products can be developed and traded.

Classification of commodities

Zooming in on the asset class commodities could lead to identify subcategories.

At further detailed level, more subclasses can be identified. Metals can be split into precious and non-precious metals.

Indirect investments

Nowadays, the ownership of shares, bonds or currencies is registered digitally.

Consequently, the transfer of title takes place without physical hassle. The physical process, however, is unavoidable with commodities. As they are consumed physically they also have to be transported materially. Analogously, storage of commodities requires physical storage capacity. Nevertheless, investors and financial traders who would like to be exposed to commodity prices typically dislike to purchase commodities physically, because then they must store the actual products. However, most of these market participants do not hold tangible storage capacity. Moreover, most of them do not want to be involved with the relevant concrete matters at all. This is why investments are made indirectly. Luckily for them, exposures can be created in many ways.

Indirect investments in commodities can be made by placing capital in equity.

One could, for instance, buy shares of mining firms, oil and gas companies or corporates which produce or process agricultural products. However, this brings risk beyond commodity prices. After all, a stock price is not just influenced by the relevant commodity price. Moreover, a corporate share price is impacted by numerous drivers, amongst which are the management, logistical success or failures and operational performance, but also the management and possibly even accounting scandals. This often leads to a discrepancy between the stock price development and the underlying commodity price development. This basis risk could work two ways, namely in favour or adversely. One could profit from leverage but, on the other side, one may want to avoid underperformance. Therefore, investors often seek an alternative indirect investment opportunity, with a more direct relationship. Commodity derivatives provide such an alternative. A commodity derivatives contract is an agreement whereby the underlying value typically concerns a commodity or commodity index. Examples of commodity derivatives are commodity futures, commodity options and commodity swaps.

Commodity markets are complex systems

Before taking a position in commodities, an investor or market participant has to realise that the commodity markets are much more complex than capital markets, FX markets or money markets. After all, commodity markets face most elements that drive and influence typical financial markets, but on top of that, commodity markets are severely impacted by many more driving forces, such as politics, weather circumstances and the availability plus utilisation of production, consumption, transport and storage capacity. For this reason, one requires in-depth knowledge about technical aspects. A background in engineering or physics would be quite helpful to understand the commodity supply chains and, hence, the commodity markets. Compared to the money markets, commodity markets are relatively new, and thus far from mature. In addition, they face relatively many fundamental price driving factors, they are significantly impacted by economic cycles and they are typically exposed to a relatively large number of events. As a consequence of the latter, commodity prices face relatively high volatility, especially in the spot markets. Moreover, some commodity markets can even show negative prices. In addition, commodity markets, compared to money markets, are characterised by a relatively weak relationship between spot and forward prices, have to deal with strong seasonality, show fragmented markets instead of centralisation and face relatively complex derivatives.

CHAPTER 22:

Application on the Crypto Value Market

The query whether crypto-currencies follow structured chart behaviors similar to the normal economic markets has been presented by several traders. Admittedly, crypto-currencies similar to Bitcoin and Ethereum act very well owing to the dearth of elementary players whose supposition can be opposite to the actual behavior of crypto-currency prices. These charts are unpredictable when it comes to fluctuation of price but can be effective as far as the prediction of the potential behavior of price is concerned.

The effective representation of basic graphical patterns across this period is evident from left to right side of the graph.

The upper points on the graph show the breakout of a falling wedge to determine the initial point of the wedge.

The breakout of the consolidation zone is directed upwards. The target is labeled thus stopping the move.

The upper target estimated by the block keeps the trend moving upwards leading to fulfillment and beginning of a stronger pullback.

The breakout of the rising wedge is directed towards the downside. The results are indicated in the next chart.

The breakout of the rising wedge is followed by the pullback from an extended move.

A measured move target that is ready is likely to bring about the multi down leg.

The measured move target can also be achieved by the tagged wedge break target. This eliminates the need to go low.

As the falling wedge is considered unusual pattern of topping, there was an expectation of year-high test.

The step by step explanation is given to facilitate your understanding.

The fundamental graphical pattern will represent the reasonable forecasting power on near-term price movements, as long as a standardized market exists for the trading of any instrument. In other words, if the trader is only focused on his profits, the graph pattern will depict the expected outcomes of market behavior. Since different types of people are engaged in crypto-currency trade and financial markets, it's obvious that the fluctuation of price will also be different for both types of trades.

Due to the introduction of futures contracts on Bitcoin, however this situation is changing. This enables the experienced trade firm employees to trade crypto-currencies under the protective regulations offered by various exchanges such as Chicago Board of Trade and the Chicago Mercantile Exchange. It is expected that the huge financial organizations will shortly take over the current crypto-currency players.

To sum it up, Bitcoin is expected to act similar to a developing regulated derivatives market. Due to the possible use of arbitrage algorithms for trading Bitcoin with financial institutes, greater correspondence is seen between the price actions of the bitcoin and other financial markets. Contrary to the claims of bitcoin promoters, bitcoin is now becoming the financial tool intended to serve a particular purpose.

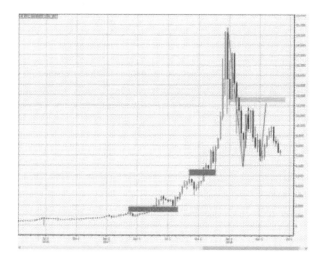

The next move of the bitcoin is still the main query forwarded by many after it deviated from the ever-high of 19666. It must amaze many that the stock market bottom with S&P 500 is printing a low of 666. The main thing here is not if there is any conspiracy involved behind this and we will only focus on the facts depicted from charts.

The chart shown above shows the Bitcoin details.

In year 2017, a couple of pockets were left behind by the massive upwards movement towards the blow-off. It was expected that the higher one will be tagged; however, it did not occur till now. This implies that Bitcoin is still expected to trade between 5500 and 5600 prior to trading over 12600 which was its level at 2017 closing.

The movement of the bitcoin to the 2017 closure of 12600 from the existing level of trading over 7000 (May 2018) will be considered as the complex multiple leg move. This movement is expected to be followed with immediate selling most probably targeting the low pockets.

Considering the time taken by the bitcoin to move above 19000, it is logical to expect the bitcoin to require similar time period to grasp this move.

It is appropriate to check the bottoming of the bitcoin as long as there is no formation of weekly level bottom pattern. Although it may require a lot of patience by Perma bulls to wait for the bottoming of bitcoin, it is worth waiting since it may fell down boundlessly.

Ethereum

The peak of the bitcoin was followed by the peak of various other crypto-currencies particularly Ethereum which showed a rise to maximum position in January 2018. This may be attributed to the hype created by Bitcoin at that time. More interesting is the fact that Ethereum doubled even after the fall of bitcoin. Such a movement was new for the Ethereum however; bitcoin has seen this up and down many times.

Three downside pushes are evident from the Ethereum's pullback structure. The Ethereum put an end to this move prior to reaching the third downside target. This was done through the resistance trend line's breakout shown by an upward arrow.

The breakout lead to an upwards move towards the peak of the channel due to the swing lows developed in the pullback process.

It resulted in a situation where second swing held more importance. Currently, Ethereum is being traded at this zone (as at end of May 2018).

In case of maintenance of this level, we can expect an upward move towards the start of the pullback as per the indication of the three pushes down pattern. The highest-ever level of Ethereum is the start of pullback. The potential situation of the bitcoin is different from this situation of Ethereum.

However, this is not that simple. The daily charts still reveal a downtrend with a strong resistance being shown by the down channel top. Ethereum will not move upwards and will be kept low as long as the channel top is not cleared. The channel top will cause the Ethereum to break the record of the lowest level made in May 2018. Keeping the channel midpoint as the main target, even lower prices are expected. Currently (as of end of May 2018), the mid-channel level is almost 300.

Crypto-Currency is Not Money

In my opinion I must clarify the fact that crypto-currencies would not be able to rule the world in their current position as claimed by their promoters. They are not a valuable source or a monetary form. Although the concept of the significance of the crypto-currency for restoring trust was reasonable, it could not yield the desired results because of technological issues and issues in practical execution. However, no significant harm was caused to the assets.

The longing to make money from technological advancements led to the emergence of various ideas. In particular, the advent of crypto-currencies is expected to bring revolutions in the future transactions. It is expected that the crypto-currency concept will bring about technological advancements causing massive revolutions in all aspects.

It is not easy to determine the crypto-currency that can endure the current bearish market trends. Even if one determines the right kind of crypto-currency, it is expected to lose its significance with the technological advancements in the similar manner in which the advent of Facebook rendered the previous social media platforms as obsolete.

Trading in crypto-currencies must involve a lot of caution on part of the trader since it is a hazardous play. It is better to understand the risky nature of crypto-currencies so that you don't put the amount you cannot afford to lose for betting. This statement is right for all types of trades. There is no emphasis on the management of risk to be the only factor of concern for the survival of a trader in this market.

CHAPTER 23:

Top Day Trading Tools

Software Tools

Retail traders, in particular, can already access almost the same kinds of programs used by institutional traders. Moreover, many of these tools are either available online or downloadable in the computer. In fact, with the growing popularity of mobile devices such as tablets and smart phones, some of these programs can also be downloaded in these devices. This way, you can trade anytime and anywhere even when you're on a holiday or commuting.

These software tools can include:

Stock Screeners

A stock screener is a tool that allows you to compare company stocks against a set of criteria, which can include share price, market capitalization, dividend yield, volatility, valuation ratios, and analyst estimates.

What I like about stock screeners is they are very easy to use since the parameters can already be provided for you. All you have to do is to choose.

Now I can get more information on every company or narrow my search some more so I have fewer but hopefully better-choice stocks to consider.

Stock screeners can be an excellent tool too to begin your research. In fact, it guides you on what kind of information to look for as you can see in the MORE INFO column. You can save more time as well. Note, though, that not all stock screeners have the same features. Some are pretty basic while others are comprehensive they can also let you run screening for other types of securities like bonds and mutual funds, like Yahoo Finance.

Auto Traders

Also known as automatic trading systems, these are programs that execute buys and sells on your behalf. Normally, you just set certain parameters, and they do the rest. One of the biggest advantages of auto trading is you don't have to constantly keep track of your trading literally as the system does it for you. In fact, over the years, it has become more sophisticated that it can already "read" historical data and provide you with recommendations or information so you can make more correct decisions. Also, you can execute the same commands multiple times in any given day and trade several accounts or orders at any given time.

However, there are downsides. First, there's disruption of the markets. In 2014 over 70% of trading is due to these automated systems. Now imagine if every trader executes huge orders every single time. Market movements can then become incredibly erratic. Moreover, even if these systems are designed to work more powerfully than any trader's thinking and analytical capacity, they are still prone to glitches, and these glitches can be disastrous. For example, it can place large orders that you don't want to in the first place.

Streaming Quotes

You can also consider this as your equivalent to a ticker tape. The only difference is that you'll get more information from streaming quotes.

Now streaming quotes are quotes displayed in real time, so don't be surprised if the numbers tend to change very fast for certain stocks. It only goes to show that the market is definitely active. For a day trader, streaming quotes are a valuable tool as they can help you make decisions including corrections on the fly. You can spot emerging buying and selling trends and analyze real-time charts. NASDAQ has an example of a streaming quote, although it's much simpler than the others like Quotestream or Scottrader.

Live Market Analysis

Although technical analysis is essential in day trading, you should also not neglect fundamental analysis as the latter can even dictate the results of the former. For this reason, I also use Live Market Analysis.

Live Market Analysis is simply a collection of any information, news, press releases, and reports pertaining to the companies that are being traded. They may not be directly related to finance (e.g., news about mergers or acquisitions) but they can influence stock price movement within the day.

You can source the analysis online such as Yahoo or Google Finance.

Stop Loss Management

I hope I've already established the fact that stop loss is incredibly important as part of your risk management strategy.

Learning Markets gives us two more options. These are the support and moving average methods.

Support levels refer to the level in which stock price dips the lowest before it goes high up. When you look at a fall below the uptrend is the support level. In the support method, your stop loss can be placed just a bit below than the previous support level as this assumes that going below the stop-loss price means a continuous or longer downtrend for the stock.

Investopedia, on the other hand, has a good definition of moving averages. One of the benefits of this is that it cancels out "noise" or fluctuations that may not be that consistent. In other words, it gives you a clear picture of the possible movement of stock prices. For the stop loss setup, you can determine the moving average and have it just below the moving average.

Penny Stock Level 2 Quotes

Once in a while, day traders look for a penny stock, although the name can be a misnomer since, according to the Securities and Exchange Commission (SEC), these stocks are those that have less than $5 per share value.

Some traders like penny stocks because there's a lot of room for appreciation, which means opportunities for massive return. Moreover, a person's capital can go a long way with penny stocks. For example, if a person has $5,000, he can allocate $1,000 for penny stocks worth $3 each. This means he gets 300 shares (rounded off to the nearest hundreds). Compare that if he uses the same amount to buy shares worth $5.

However, there are several downsides with penny stocks. One, they are hard to come by and they are thinly traded. Therefore, there's not much technical information you can use to make good decisions about them. Second, they are usually not found in major exchanges because they have failed to meet some of the requirements or criteria. You may also have issues with liquidity, which means you may not be able to sell the stock quickly simply because penny stocks themselves are not that liquid.

Nevertheless, if you want to give penny stocks a try, you can use Level 2 Quotes, which is obviously higher than the level 1 quote, which includes the streaming quote. An important data available in level 2 quote is that of the market maker or those who have significant control of the market, including the brokerage firms. They are the ones who have massive volumes of order sizes, which they are going to trade. Market makers meant to earn a profit, so orders may be hold off until they know they can make a gain. Traders in level 1, however, wouldn't know that. In level 2 quotes, traders can observe movements of money makers and see what stocks they have the most interest.

CHAPTER 24:

Momentum Trading

Momentum is at the heart of all-day trading as finding trades with the right amount of momentum is the only way you can reliably guarantee a profit on your trades. Luckily, it is not unrealistic to expect to find at least one underlying asset that is likely to move as much as 30 percent each day due to the fact that all underlying assets with this much momentum all tend to share a few common technical indicators.

Momentum stock anatomy

While it might seem difficult to understand how anyone could expect to pick a stock with the right momentum out of the thousands of possible choices, the fact of the matter is that all high momentum stocks typically have several things in common. In fact, if you were given a list of 5,000 stocks, using the factors below you could likely come up with a list of 10 or less.

Float: The first thing you are going to want to keep in mind is that the stocks with the highest momentum are generally going to have a float that is less than 100 million shares. Float refers to the total number of shares that are currently available and can be found by taking the total number of outstanding shares and subtracting out all those that are restricted or are, functionally speaking, no longer traded. Restricted shares are those that are currently in the midst of a lockup period or other, similar restriction. The less float a stock has, the more volatility it is going to contain. Stocks with smaller float tend to have low liquidity and a higher bid/ask spread.

Daily charts: The next thing you are going to want to look for is stocks that are consistently beating their moving average and trending away from either the support or resistance depending on if you following a positive or negative trend.

Relative volume: You are also going to want to ensure that the stocks you are considering have a high amount of relative volume, with the minimum being twice what the current average is. The average you should consider in this case would be the current volume compared to the historical average for the stock in question. The standard volume is going to reset every night at midnight which means this is a great indicator when it comes to stocks that are seeing a higher than average amount of action right now.

Catalyst: While not, strictly speaking, required, you may still find it helpful to look for stocks that are currently having their momentum boosted by external sources. This can include things like activist investors, FDA announcements, and PR campaigns and earnings reports.

Exit indicators to watch

Besides knowing what a potentially profitable momentum trade looks like, you are also going to need to know what to look for to ensure that you can successfully get while the getting is good. Keep the following in mind and you will always be able to get out without having to sacrifice any of your hard earned profits.

Don't get greedy: It is important to set profit targets before you go into any trade, and then follow through on them when the trade turns in your favor. If you find yourself riding a stronger trend than you initially anticipated, the best choice is to instead sell off half of your holdings before setting a new and improved price target for the rest, allowing you to have your cake and eat it too.

Red candles: If you are not quite at your price target and you come across a candle that closes in the red then this is a strong indicator that you should take what you have and exit ASAP. If you have already sold off half of your holdings at this point, however, then you are going to want to go ahead and hold through the first red candle as long as it doesn't go so far as to actively trigger your stop loss.

Extension bar: An extension bar is a candle with a spike that causes dramatically increased profits. If this occurs you want to lock in your profits as quickly as possible as it is unlikely to last very long. This is your lucky day and it is important to capitalize on it.

Choosing a screener

Another important aspect of using a momentum strategy correctly is using a quality stock screen in order to find stocks that are trending towards the extreme ends of the market based on the criteria outlined above. A good screener is a virtually indispensable tool when it comes to narrowing down the field of potential options on any given day, the best of the best even let you generate your own unique filters that display a list of stocks that meet a variety of different criteria. What follows is a list of some of the most popular screeners on the market today.

StockFetchter: StockFetcher is one of the more complicated screeners out there, but all that complexity comes with a degree of power that is difficult to beat. Its power comes from a virtually unlimited number of parameters that its users can add to filter, ensuring that you only see exactly the types of stocks you are looking for. It offers a free as well as a paid version, the free version allows you to see the top five stocks that match your parameters while the paid version, $8.95 per month, shows you unlimited results.

Finviz: This site offers a wide variety of different premade filters that are designed to return results on the most promising stocks for a given day. It is extremely user friendly as well and functions from three drop-down menus based on the type of indicator, technical, fundamental or descriptive, and lets you choose the criteria for each. The results can then be sorted in a myriad of different ways to make it as easy to find the types of stocks you are looking for as possible. The biggest downside to Finviz is that it uses delayed data which means it is going to be most effective for those who run evening screens so they are ready to go when the market opens.

Chartmill: This site allows users to filter stocks based on a number of predetermined criteria including things like price, performance, volume, technical indicators and candlestick patterns. It also offers up a number of more specialized indicators including things like squeeze plays, intensity, trend and pocket pivots. This site works based on a credit system, and every user is given 6,000 credits each month for free. Every scan costs a few hundred credits so you should be able to take advantage of a variety of their tools virtually free of charge. Additional credits then cost $10 per 10,000 or they have an unlimited option available for about $30 per month.

Stockrover^l: This tool is specifically designed to cater to the Canadian market in addition to the US stock market. It offers up a variety of fundamental filters in addition to technical and performance-based options. This tool also allows you to track stocks that are near their established lows and high, those that may be gaining momentum and even those that are seeing a lot of love from various hedge funds. Users also have the ability to create custom screens as well as unique equations for even more advanced screening. Users can also backtest their ideas to make sure that everything is working as intended. While their basic options are free to use, the more complex choices are gated behind a paywall that costs $250 for a year's subscription.

Know your filters

Day trading is about more than finding stocks that are high in volume, it is also about finding those that are currently experiencing a higher than average degree of movement as well. The following filters will help ensure that the stocks you find have plenty of both.

Steady volatility: In order to trade stocks that are extremely volatile with as little research as possible, the following criterion is a good place to start. While additional research is always going to be preferable in the long run, you can find success if you run this scan once a week and pay close attention to the results. This list should ideally return stocks that have moved at least 5 percent every day for the past 50 days. It is important to use a minimum of 50 days, though 75 or 100 will produce even more reliable results overall. Results of this magnitude will show that the stock in question has moved a significant amount over the past few months which means it is likely to continue to do so for the near future. The second criterion will determine the amount you should be willing to pay per share and can be altered based on your personal preferences.

The third criterion will determine the level of volume that you find acceptable for the given timeframe. The example will look for volume that is greater than four million shares within the past month. From there, it will eliminate leverage ETFs from the results which can be eliminated if you are interested in trading ETFs. Finally, the add column will show the list of stocks with the largest amount of volume and the greatest overall amount of movement. Selecting these columns will then rank the results from least to greatest based on the criteria provided.

Monitor regularly: Alternately, you may want to do a daily search to determine the stocks that will experience the greatest range of movement in the coming hours. To do so, you will want to create a new list of stocks every evening to ensure that you will be ready to go when the market opens. This list can then be made up of stocks that have shown a higher volatility in the previous day either in terms of gains or in terms of losses. Adding in volume to these criteria will then help to make sure the results will likely continue to generate the kind of volume that day trading successfully requires. Useful filters for this search include an average volume that is greater than one million and the more you increase the minimum volume the fewer results you'll see.

When using this strategy, it is especially important to pick out any stocks that are likely to see major news releases before the next day as these are almost guaranteed to make the price move in a number of random directions before ultimately settling down. As such, it is often best to wait until after the details of the release are known and you can more accurately determine what the response is, though not so long that you miss out on the combination of high volume and high volatility. If you don't already have an earnings calendar bookmarked, the one available for free from Yahoo Finance! Is well respected.

Monitor intraday volatility: Another option that is worth considering is doing your researching during the day as a means of determining which stocks are experiencing the greatest overall amount of movement at the moment.

CHAPTER 25:

Common Day Trading Mistakes to Avoid

A side from doing the right things, you'll also need to refrain from certain things to succeed as a day trader. Here are some of the most common day trading mistakes you should avoid committing.

Excessive Day Trading

By excessive, I mean executing too many day trades. One of the most common mistakes many newbie day traders make is assuming that they can become day trading ninjas in just a couple of weeks if they trade often enough to get it right. But while more practice can eventually translate into day trading mastery later on, it doesn't mean you can cram all that practice in a very short period of time via very frequent day trading. The adage "the more, the merrier" doesn't necessarily apply to day trading.

Remember, timing is crucial for day trading success. And timing is dependent on how the market is doing during the day. There will be days when day trading opportunities are few and far between and there'll be days when day trading opportunities abound. Don't force trades for the sake of getting enough day trades under your belt.

Even in the midst of a plethora of profitable day trading opportunities, the more the merrier still doesn't apply. Why? If you're a newbie trader, your best bet at becoming a day trading ninja at the soonest possible time is to concentrate on one or two day trades per day only. By limiting your day trades, to just one or two, you have the opportunity to closely monitor and learn from your trades.

Can you imagine executing 5 or more trades daily as a newbie and monitor all those positions simultaneously? You'll only get confused and overwhelmed and worse, you may even miss day trading triggers and signals and fail to profitably close your positions.

Winging It

If you want to succeed as a day trader, you need to hold each trading day in reverence and high esteem. How do you do that? By planning your day trading strategies for the day and executing those strategies instead of just winging it.

As cliché as it may sound, failing to plan really is planning to fail. And considering the financial stakes involved in day trading, you shouldn't go through your trading days without any plan on hand. Luck favors those who are prepared and planning can convince lady luck that you are prepared.

Expecting Too Much Too Soon

This much is true about day trading: it's one of the most exciting and exhilarating jobs in the world! And stories many day traders tell of riches accumulated through this economic activity add more excitement, desire, and urgency for many to get into it.

However, too much excitement and desire resulting from many day trading success stories can be very detrimental to newbie day traders. Let me correct myself: it is detrimental to newbie day traders. Why?

Such stories, many of which are probably urban legends, give newbies unrealistic expectations of quick and easy day trading riches. Many beginner day traders get the impression that day trading is a get-rich-quick scheme!

It's not. What many day traders hardly brag about are the times they also lost money and how long it took them to master the craft enough to quit their jobs and do it full time. And even rarer are stories of the myriad number of people who've attempted day trading and failed. It's the dearth of such stories that tend to make day trading neophytes have unrealistic expectations about day trading.

What's the problem with lofty day trading expectations? Here's the problem: if you have very unrealistic expectations, it's almost certain that you'll fail. It's because unrealistic expectations can't be met and therefore, there's zero chances for success.

One of the most unrealistic expectations surrounding day trading is being able to double one's initial trading capital in a couple of months, at most. Similar to such expectations is that of being able to quit one's day job and live an abundant life in just a few months via day trading.

Successful day traders went through numerous failures, too, before they succeeded at day trading and were able to do it for a living.

If you decide to give day trading a shot, have realistic expectations. In fact, don't even expect to profit soon. Instead take the initial losses as they come, limiting them through sensible stop-loss limits, and learning from them. Eventually, you'll get the hang of it and your day trading profits will start eclipsing your day trading losses.

Changing Strategies Frequently

Do you know how to ride a bike? If not, do you know someone who does? Whether it's you or somebody you know, learning how to ride a bike wasn't instant. It took time and a couple of falls and bruises along the way.

But despite falls, scratches and bruises, you or that person you know stuck to learning how to ride a bike and with enough time and practice, succeeded in doing so. It was because you or the other person knew that initial failures mean that riding a bike was impossible. It's just challenging at first.

It's the same with learning how to day trade profitably. You'll need to give yourself enough time and practice to master it. Just because you suffered trading losses in the beginning doesn't mean it's not working or it's not for you. It probably means you haven't really mastered it yet.

But if you quit and shift to a new trading strategy or plan quickly, you'll have to start again from scratch, extend your learning time, and possibly lose more money than you would've if you stuck around to your initial strategy long enough to give yourself a shot at day trading successfully or concluding with certainty that it's not working for you.

If you frequently change your day trading strategies, i.e., you don't give yourself enough time to learn day trading strategies, your chances of mastering them become much lower. In which case, your chances of succeeding in day trading becomes much lower, too.

Not Analyzing Past Trades

Those who don't learn history are doomed to repeat it, said writer and philosopher George Santayana. We can paraphrase it to apply to day traders, too: Those who don't learn from their day trading mistakes will be doomed to repeat them.

If you don't keep a day trading journal containing records of all your trades and more importantly, analyze them, you'll be doomed to repeat your losing day trades. It's because by not doing so, you won't be able to determine what you're doing wrong and what you should be doing instead in order to have more profitable day trades than losing ones.

As another saying goes: if you always do what you always did, you'll always get what you always got. Unless you analyze your past day trades on a regular basis, you'll be doomed to repeating the same mistakes and continue losing money on them.

Ditching Correlations

We can define correlations as a relationship where one thing influences the outcome or behavior of another. A positive correlation means that both tend to move in the same direction or exhibit similar behaviors, i.e., when one goes up, the other goes up, too, and vice versa.

Correlations abound in the stock market. For example, returns on the stock market are usually negatively correlated with the Federal Reserve's interest rates, i.e., when the Feds increase interest rates, returns on stock market investments go down and vice versa.

Correlations exist across industries in the stock market, too. For example, property development stocks are positively correlated to steel and cement manufacturing stocks. This is because when the property development's booming, it buys more steel and cement from manufacturing companies, which in turn also increase their income.

Ignoring correlations during day trading increase your risks for erroneous position taking and exiting. You may take a short position on a steel manufacturer's stock while taking a long position on a property development company's stock and if they have a positive correlation, one of those two positions will most likely end up in a loss.

But caution must be exercised with using correlations in your day trades. Don't establish correlations where there's none. Your job is to simply identify if there are observable correlations, what those correlations are, and how strong they are.

Being Greedy

Remember the story of the goose that lay golden eggs? Because the goose's owner was so greedy and couldn't wait for the goose to lay more eggs immediately, he killed the goose and cut it open.

Sadly for the owner, there were no golden eggs inside the goose because it only created and laid one golden egg every day. His greed caused him to destroy his only wealth-generating asset.

When it comes to day trading, greed can have the same negative financial impact. Greed can make a day trader hold on to an already profitable position longer than needed and result in smaller profits later on or worse, trading losses.

If you remember my story, that was greed in action. Had I been content with the very good returns I already had and closed my position, my paper gains could've become actual gains. I let my greed control my trading and chose to hold on to that stock much longer than I needed to. That trade turned into a losing one eventually.

That's why you must be disciplined enough to stick to your day trading stop-loss and profit-taking limits. And that's why you should program those limits on your platform, too. Doing so minimizes the risks of greed hijacking your otherwise profitable day trades.

CHAPTER 26:

Portfolio Diversification

D
ay traders generally execute trades in the course of a single trading day while investors buy and hold stocks for days, weeks, months, and sometimes even a couple of years. In between these two extremes are other forms of trading. These include swing trading and position trading, among others.

Swing trading is where a trader buys an interest in a commodity or stock and holds the position for a couple of days before disposing of it. Position trading, on the other hand, is where a trader buys a stake in a commodity or stock for a number of weeks or even several months. While all these trades carry a certain element of risk, day trading carries the biggest risk.

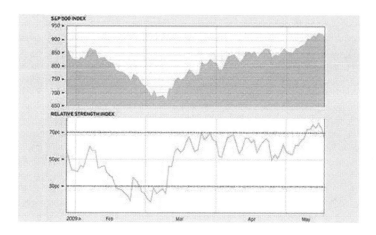

A trader with the necessary skills and access to all the important resources is bound to succeed and will encounter a steep learning curve. Professional day traders work full time, whether working for themselves or for large institutions. They often set a schedule which they always adhere to. It is never wise to be a part-time day trader, a hobby trader, or a gambler. To succeed, you have to trade on a fulltime basis and be as disciplined as possible.

Introduction to Diversification

Diversification is considered an effective risk management technique. It is widely used by both traders and investors. The gist behind this approach is that investing funds in just single security is extremely risky as the entire trade could potentially go up in smoke or incur significant losses.

An ideal portfolio of securities is expected to fetch a much higher return compared to a no-diversified portfolio. This is true even when compared to the returns of lower risk investments like bonds. Generally, diversification is advisable not only because it yields better returns but also because it offers protection against losses.

Diversification Basics

Traders and investors put their funds in securities at the securities markets. One of the dangers of investing in the markets is that traders are likely to hold onto only one or two stocks at a time. This is risky because if a trade was to fail, then the trader could experience a catastrophe. However, with diversification, the risk is spread out so that regardless of what happens to some stocks, the trader still stands to be profitable.

At the core of diversification is the challenge posed by unsystematic risks. When some stocks or investments perform better than others, these risks are neutralized. Therefore, for a perfectly balanced portfolio, a trader should ensure that they only deal with assets that are non-correlated. This means that the assets respond in opposite ways or differently to market forces.

The ideal portfolio should contain between 25 and 30 different securities. This is the perfect way of ensuring that the risk levels are drastically reduced and the only expected outcomes are profitability.

In summary, diversification is a popular strategy that is used by both traders and investors. It makes use of a wide variety of securities in order to improve yield and mitigate against inherent and potential risks.

It is advisable to invest or trade in a variety of assets and not all from one class. For instance, a properly diversified portfolio should include assets such as currencies, options, stocks, bonds, and so on. This approach will increase the chances of profitability and minimize risks and exposure. Diversification is even better if assets are acquired across geographical regions as well.

Best Diversification Approach

Diversification focuses on asset allocation. It consists of a plan that endeavors to allocate funds or assets appropriately across a variety of investments. When an investor diversifies his or her portfolio, then there is some level of risk that has to be accepted. However, it is also advisable to devise an exit strategy so that the investor is able to let go of the asset and recoup their funds. This becomes necessary when a specific asset class is not yielding any worthwhile returns compared to others.

If an investor is able to create an aptly diversified portfolio, their investment will be adequately covered. An adequately diversified portfolio also allows room for growth. Appropriate asset allocation is highly recommended as it allows investors a chance to leverage risk and manage any possible portfolio volatility because different assets have varying reactions to adverse market conditions.

Investor opinions on diversifications

Different investors have varying opinions regarding the type of investment scenarios they consider being ideal. Numerous investors believe that a properly diversified portfolio will likely bring in a double-digit return despite prevailing market conditions. They also agree that in the worst case situation will be simply a general decrease in the value of the different assets. Yet with all this information out there, very few investors are actually able to achieve portfolio diversification.

So why are investors unable to simply diversify their portfolios appropriately? The answers are varied and diverse. The challenges encountered by investors in diversification include weighting imbalance, hidden correlation, underlying devaluation, and false returns, among others. While these challenges sound rather technical, they can easily be solved. The solution is also rather simple. By hacking these challenges, an investor will then be able to benefit from an aptly diversified platform.

The Process of Asset Class Allocation

There are different ways of allocating investments to assets. According to studies, most investors, including professional investors, portfolio managers, and seasoned traders actually rarely beat the indexes within their preferred asset class. It is also important to note that there is a visible correlation between the performance of an underlying asset class and the returns that an investor receives. In general, professional investors tend to perform more or less the same as an index within the same class asset.

Investment returns from a diversified portfolio can generally be expected to closely imitate the related asset class. Therefore, asset class choice is considered an extremely crucial aspect of an investment. In fact, it is the single more crucial aspect for the success of a particular asset class. Other factors, such as individual asset selection and market timing, only contribute about 6% of the variance in investment outcomes.

Wide Diversifications between Various Asset Classes

Diversification to numerous investors simply implies spreading their funds through a wide variety of stocks in different sectors such as health care, financial, energy, as well as medium caps, small, and large-cap companies. This is the opinion of your average investor. However, a closer look at this approach reveals that investors are simply putting their money in different sectors of stocks class. These asset classes can very easily fall and rise when the markets do.

A reliably diversified portfolio is one where the investor or even the manager is watchful and alert because of the hidden correlation that exists between different asset classes. This correlation can easily change with time, and there are several reasons for this. One reason is international markets. Many investors often choose to diversify their portfolios with international stocks.

However, there is also a noticeable correlation across the different global financial markets. This correlation is clearly visible not just across European markets but also emerging markets from around the world. There is also a clear correlation between equities and fixed income markets, which are generally the hallmarks of diversification.

This correlation is actually a challenge and is probably a result of the relationship between structured financing and investment banking. Another factor that contributes to this correlation is the rapid growth and popularity of hedge funds. Take the case where a large international organization such as a hedge fund suffers losses in a particular asset class.

Should this happen, then the firm may have to dispose of some assets across the different asset classes. This will have a multiplier effect as numerous other investments, and other investors will, therefore, be affected even though they had diversified their portfolios appropriately. This is a challenge that affects numerous investors who are probably unaware of its existence. They are also probably unaware of how it should be rectified or avoided.

Realignment of Asset Classes

One of the best approaches to solving the correlation challenge is to focus on class realignment. Basically, asset allocation should not be considered as a static process. Asset class imbalance is a phenomenon that occurs when the securities markets develop, and different asset classes exhibit varied performance.

After a while, investors should assess their investments then diversify out of underperforming assets and instead shift this investment to other asset classes that are performing well and are profitable in the long term. Even then, it is advisable to be vigilant so that no one single asset class is overweighted as other standard risks are still inherent. Also, a prolonged bullish market can result in overweighting one of the different asset classes which could be ready for a correction. There are a couple of approaches that an investor can focus on, and these are discussed below.

Diversification and the Relative Value

Investors sometimes find asset returns to be misleading, including veteran investors. As such, it is advisable to interpret asset returns in relation to the specific asset class performance. The interpretation should also take into consideration the risks that this asset class is exposed to and even the underlying currency.

When diversifying investments, it is important to think about diversifying into asset classes that come with different risk profiles. These should also be held in a variety of currencies. You should not expect to enjoy the same outcomes when investing in government bonds and technology stocks. However, it is recommended to endeavor to understand how each suits the larger investment objective.

Using such an approach, it will be possible to benefit more from a small gain from an asset within a market where the currency is increasing in value. This is as compared to a large gain from an asset within a market where the currency is in decline. As such, huge gains can translate into losses when the gains are reverted back to the stronger currency. This is the reason why it is advisable to ensure that proper research and evaluation of different asset classes are conducted.

Currencies should be considered

Currency considerations are crucial when selecting asset classes to diversify in. take the Swiss franc for instance. It is one of the world's most stable currencies and has been that way since the 1940s. Because of this reason, this particular currency can be safely and reliably used to measure the performance of other currencies.

However, private investors sometimes take too long choosing and trading stocks. Such activities are both overwhelming and time-consuming. This is why, in such instances, it is advisable to approach this differently and focus more on the asset class. With this kind of approach, it is possible to be even more profitable. Proper asset allocation is crucial to successful investing. It enables investors to mitigate any investment risks as well as portfolio volatility. The reason is that different asset classes have different reactions to all the different market conditions.

Constructing a well-thought out and aptly diversified portfolio, it is possible to have a stable and profitable portfolio that even outperforms the index of assets. Investors also have the opportunity to leverage against any potential risks because of different reactions by the different market conditions.

CHAPTER 27:

Options Day Trading Rules for Success

There is more to options day trading to just having a style or a strategy. If that was all it took, then you could just adopt those that are proven to work and just stick with them. Yes, options day trading styles and strategy are important but they are not the end-all-be-all of this career.

The winning factor is the options day trader himself or herself. You are the factor that determines whether or not you will win or lose in this career. Only taking the time to develop your expertise, seeking guidance when necessary and being totally dedicated allows a person to move from a novice options day trader to an experienced one that is successful and hitting his or her target goals.

To develop into the options day trader you want to be, being disciplined is necessary. There are options day trading rules that can help you develop that necessary discipline. You will make mistakes. Every beginner in any niche does and even experienced options day traders are human and thus, have bad days too.

Knowing common mistakes helps you avoid many of these mistakes and takes away much of the guesswork. Having rules to abide by helps you avoid these mistakes as well.

Below, I have listed 11 rules that every options day trader must know. Following them is entirely up to you but know that they are proven to help beginner options day trader turn into winning options day traders.

Rule for Success #1 – Have Realistic Expectations

It is sad to say that many people who enter the options trading industry are doing so to make a quick buck. Options trading is not a get-rich-quick scheme. It is a reputable career that has made many people rich but that is only because these people have put in the time, effort, study and dedication to learning the craft and mastering it. Mastery does not happen overnight and beginner options day traders need to be prepared for that learning curve and to have the fortitude to stick with day trading options even when it becomes tough.

Losses are also part of the game. No trading style or strategy will guarantee gains all the time. In fact, the best options traders have a winning percentage of about 80% and a losing average of approximately 20%. That is why an options day trader needs to be a good money manager and a good risk manager. Be prepared for eventual losses and be prepared to minimize those losses.

Rule for Success #2 – Start Small to Grow a Big Portfolio

Caution is the name of the game when you just get started with day trading options. Remember that you are still learning options trading and developing an understanding of the financial market. Do not jump the gun even if you are eager. After you have practiced paper trading, start with smaller options positions and steadily grow your standing as you get a lay of the options day trading land. This strategy allows you to keep your losses to a minimum and to develop a systematic way of entering positions.

Rule for Success #3 – Know Your Limits

You may be tempted to trade as much as possible to develop a winning monthly average but that strategy will have the opposite effect and land you with a losing average.

Remember that every options trader needs careful consideration before that contract is set up. Never overtrade and tie up your investment fund.

Rule for Success #4 – Be Mentally, Physically and Emotionally Prepared Every Day

This is a mentally, physically and emotionally tasking career and you need to be able to meet the demands of this career. That means keeping your body, mind and heart in good health at all times. Ensure that you schedule time for self-care every day.

That can be as simple as taking the time to read for recreation to having elaborate self-care routine carved out in the evenings.

Not keeping your mind, heart and head in optimum health means that they are more likely to fail you.

Signs that you need to buckle up and care for yourself more diligently include being constantly tired, being short-tempered, feeling preoccupied and being easily distracted.

To ensure you perform your best every day, here a few tasks that you need to perform:

- Get the recommended amount of sleep daily. This is between 7 and 9 hours for an adult.

- Practice a balanced diet. The brain and body need adequate nutrition to work their best. Include fruits, complex carbs and veggies in this diet and reduce the consumption of processed foods.

- Eat breakfast lunch and dinner every day. Fuel your mind and body with the main meals. Eating a healthy breakfast is especially important because it helps set the tone for the rest of the day.

- Exercise regularly. Being inactive increases your risk of developing chronic diseases like heart disease, certain cancers and other terrible health consequences. Adding just a few minutes of exercise to your daily routine not only reduces those risks but also allows your brain to function better, which is a huge advantage for an options day trader.

- Drink alcohol in moderation or not at all.

- Stop smoking.

- Reduce stress contributors in your environment.

Rule for Success #5 – Do Your Homework Daily

Get up early and study the financial environment before the market opens and look at the news. This allows you to develop a daily options trading plan. The process of analyzing the financial climate before the market opens is called pre-market preparation. It is a necessary task that needs to be performed every day to asset competition and to align your overall strategy with the short-term conditions of that day.

An easy way to do this is to develop a pre-market checklist. An example of a pre-market checklist includes but is not limited to:

- Checking the individual markets that you frequently trade options in or plan to trade options in to evaluate support and resistance.
- Checking the news to assess whether events that could affect the market developed overnight.
- Assessing what other options traders are doing to determined volume and competition.
- Determining what safe exits for losing positions are.
- Considering the seasonality of certain markets are some as affected by the day of the week, the month of the year, etc.

Rule for Success #6 – Analyze Your Daily Performance

To determine if the options day trading style and strategies that you have adopted are working for you, you need to track your performance. At the most basic, this needs to be done on a daily basis by virtue of the fact that you are trading options daily. This will allow you to notice patterns in your profit and loss. This can lead to you determining the why and how of these gains and losses. These determinations lead to fine tuning your daily processes for maximum returns. These daily performance reviews allow you to also make determinations on the long-term activity of your options day trading career.

Rule for Success #7 – Do Not Be Greedy

If you are fortunate enough to make a 100% return on your investment, do not be greedy and try to reap more benefit from the position. You might have the position turn on you and you can lose everything. When and if such a rare circumstance happens to you, sell your position and take the profits.

Rule for Success #8 – Pay Attention to Volatility

Volatility speaks to how likely a price change will occur over a specific amount of time on the financial market. Volatility can work for an options day trader or against the options day trader. It all depends on what the options day trader is trying to accomplish and what his or her current position is.

There are many external factors that affect volatility and such factors include the economic climate, global events and news reports. Strangles and straddles strategies are great for use in volatile markets.

There are different types of volatility and they include:

- Price volatility, which describes how the price of an asset increases or decreases based on the supply and demand of that asset.
- Historical volatility, which is a measure of how an asset has performed over the last 12 months.

- Implied volatility, which is a measure of how an asset will perform in the future.

Rule for Success #9 – Use the Greeks

Greeks are a collection of measures that provide a gage of an option's price sensitivity in relation to other factors. Each Greek is represented by a letter from the Greek alphabet. These Greeks use complex formulas to be determined but they are the system that option pricing is based on. Even though these calculations can be complex, they can be done quickly and efficiently so that options day traders can use them as a method of advancing their trades for the most profitable position.

CHAPTER 28:

Trading With the Trend

Buying Calls

So let's get started by considering the most basic strategy of all, and that is buying a call option because you believe that the price of the stock is going to increase in the near future. Therefore the goal was buying a call option would be to purchase it at the right moment and then hope that the stock will go up so much that we are able to sell the option for a profit. This all sounds simple enough almost like something that you could never miss. Unfortunately, in practice, it's actually a lot more challenging than it sounds on paper.

The first consideration is going to be whether or not you purchase an option that is in the money or out of the money. If this strategy works maybe that is not really an important consideration provided that it's not too far out of the money. The reason that people decide to purchase out of the money options is that they are cheaper as compared to in the money options. It's also a fact that if the stock is moving in the right direction out of the money options will gain at price as well.

So if someone tells you that you can't make profits from out of the money options they are not being completely honest with you. In fact, you can make profits but it's always going to depend on how the stock is moving and the distance between your strike price and the share price.

The best strategy to use when going with out of the money options is to purchase them slightly out of the money by a dollar or two. What this does is it ensures the price of the option is going to be significantly impacted by changes in the stock price. Second, you wouldn't be purchasing a call unless there was a good chance that the share price would be moving up. So if you are close in price to the market price, and there is a reasonable amount of time until expiration, there would be a good chance that the share price would actually rise above your strike price. If that happens it could mean significant profits for you.

Of course, you can always take the risk of putting it a little bit more money upfront and investing in a call option that is already in the money. If the stock price rises, that is only going to solidify your position. You also have a little bit of insurance there. That comes from the fact that if you choose a decent strike price there is a solid chance it will stay in the money and so even if it doesn't gain much value you will be able to sell it and either not lose that much, or still make a profit.

So what are we hoping for with this strategy? The main hope would be that there is a large trend that takes off so that we can write the trend and earn a healthy profit. Since options are so sensitive to the price of the stock if such a trend occurs it's pretty easy to make decent money. The key, of course, is getting in the trend at the right time and knowing when to get out of the position.

Market Awareness

The first thing to keep in mind is what I call market awareness. This involves being aware of everything that could possibly impact the price of the underlying stock. This can mean not only paying attention to the chart of the stock, but you also need to be paying attention to the news and not just financial news. So let's take a recent example by looking at Facebook. In recent months Facebook has been constantly in the news. Some of the news has been good such as a decent earnings report. On the other hand, Facebook has been receiving some pushback from governments around the world. One of the issues that have been raised is privacy concerns. Facebook is also catching a lot of flak over its plan to create a cryptocurrency.

So here is the point. Every time one of these news items comes out, it's a potential for a trend. But there are a couple of problems with this. In many cases, you simply don't know when dramatic news is going to come out. So you have to be paying attention at all times and have your money ready to go. The best-case scenario is purchasing an option for the day before some large event. People are often reacting strongly in the markets when there is a good or bad jobs report or the GDP number is about to come out. So what you would want to do in that case is first of all pay attention to the news and see what the expectations are of all the market watchers that everyone pays attention to. Of course, they are often off the mark but it gives you some kind of idea where things might be heading. If a good jobs report is expected, then you might want to invest in an index fund such as DIA which is for the Dow Jones industrial average. One thing you know is that a good jobs report is going to send the Dow and the S&P 500 up by large amounts. So the key is to be prepared by purchasing your options the day before. But on the other hand you might be wrong with your guess, which could be costly.

You could wait until the news actually comes out. But I have to say from my experience trading this is a difficult proposition. The reason is you would be surprised how quickly the price rises when dramatic news comes out either way. So when one sense is a safer way to approach things but the price might be rising so fast that you find it nearly impossible to actually purchase the options. That you can execute a trade the trend might even be over. But if you're there in the middle of the action you might as well try and then you can ride it out and probably make pretty good profits.

Some people like to sit around and study stock market charts. During the course of everyday trading when there hasn't been any dramatic news announcement or something like that which will massively impact the price of the underlying stock, looking at candlesticks charts along with moving averages can give you a good idea of went to enter or exit trades. However, it's fair to say that there is a little bit of hype surrounding these tools. The fact is they don't always work because they are easily misled or maybe it's the human mind that is misled by short term changes that go against the main trend but is temporary. So you can make the mistake while following candlesticks and moving averages of seeing evidence of the sudden downtrend and then selling your position, only to find out that the downtrend wasn't real and it was only a temporary setback soon followed by a resumption of the main trend. So that is something to be careful about.

Setting Profit Goals

If you were going to trade this way probably the best thing to do is to set a specific level of modest profit to use as a goal. One that I use is $50 per options contract. Some people may be more conservative so you could set a goal of $30 profit. Some people might be more risk-oriented. I would honestly discourage that kind of thinking because sitting there hoping for $100 dollars profit per contract, while it is possible, you may also find yourself in a situation more often than not where you lose money. What might happen is you have to sit around waiting too long to hit that magic number and it never materializes. Options can quickly turn from winners into losers because they magnify the changes in the underlying stock price by 100. So it's very easy to lose money quickly.

In my experience, the $50 price level is pretty good. The only time that this value has hurt me is when I see the $50 profit hit and I failed to sell my positions because I got greedy watching the upward trend and hoped for even more money. So that is something you should avoid it's better to stick to your law, whatever you happen to pick, and then always implemented no matter what the situation is. Remember that there is always another day to trade. You're trading career never depends on a single trade or a single days trading. The bottom line is that it's better to take a small profit her option contract and per trade and then go back and trade some more, then it is to hope for large profits that may never materialize. Also, you can always magnify small profits by trading multiple options at once. So if you trade 10 options and you're only going to accept a $30 profit on the trade, which means in total you could make $300. It doesn't really matter what specific number you pick, but you should pick a value and stick to it. If I have a regret from trading the only regret is that I didn't stick to the rules that I have set for myself.

Day Trading?

For those who are not aware, if you are labeled a patterned day trader, you need to have $25,000 in your account, and you need to open a margin account. So for most individual traders with small accounts, the last thing you want is to be labeled as a day trader. However, since options lose a lot of value from time decay, and many trends are short-lived, you may find yourself in situations where you have to enter a day trade. But if you are doing this make sure that you only do three per five day trading period. That way you will avoid getting the designation and all the problems that might come about with it. In this case, if you buy a lot of several options that have the same strike price and the same expiration date, those are going to count as the same security. That may result in problems if you need to unload them all on the same day. One way to get around this is to purchase call options with slightly different strike prices instead of getting a bunch with all the same strike price. Of course, if you were going to hold your positions overnight and risk the loss from time decay having to do that may not be something to worry about.

Trading Puts

Trading puts using these techniques is going to be basically the same, with the only difference being that you would be looking for downward trends. This is actually a little bit different because people are accustomed to thinking in terms of rising stock prices means profits. So it might be hard to wrap your mind around the idea of profiting from stock market declines.

Conclusion

Thank you for making it through to the end of Day Trading Strategies, let's hope it was informative and able to provide you with all of the tools and information you need to manage your journey in the market trade.

Day trading is described as the process of speculation of risks and either buying or selling of financial instruments on the same day of trading. The financial instruments are bought at a lower price and later sold at a higher price. People who participate in this form of trade are mostly referred to as speculators. Day trading is the different form of trading known as swing trading. Swing trading involves selling of financial instruments and latter buying them at a lower price. It is a form of trade that has several people have invested their time and capital in. The potential for making profits is very high. However, it is also accompanied by the high potential of making huge percentages of loss. People who are terms as high-risk takers have the potential to realize good amounts of profits or huge losses. It is because of the nature of the trade. The losses are experienced because of several variables that are always present in trading. The gains and individual experiences are brought to light by margin buying.

There as a big difference between swing trade and day trade. The difference hails from their definitions, it goes a mile ahead to time spent in and risks involvement in both forms of trade. Day trade has lower risk involvement but one has to spend more of his or her time, unlike swing trade. Day traders are prone to participating in two forms of trade which are long trades or short trades. Long trade involves an individual purchasing the financial instruments and selling them after them increasing in value. On the other hand, short trade involves selling financial instruments and later purchasing them after their prices have dropped.

The trading market has undergone through several advancements. The major change was witnessed during the deregulation process. There was the creation of electronic financial markets during this period. One of the major innovations was the high-frequency trading index. It uses heavy algorithms to enable huge financial firms in stock trading to perform numerous orders in seconds. It is advantageous because it can also predict market trends.

The process of day trading has several challenges. An individual is supposed to be able to make a good decision during two important moments. The first moment is during a good streak and the other is during moments an individual has a poor run. At this point risk management and trading, psychology comes in handy to help an individual in the trade. One is not supposed to panic or make hasty decisions during these moments. It is important for an individual to have an effective watchlist. A good watchlist built by a trader is supposed to be able to understand the modern trading markets. This is made possible when it features stocks in play, float and market capital, pre-market grippers, real-time intraday scans, and planning trade based on scanners. The success of day trading is also incumbent on effective strategies. The common strategies include ABCD patterns, bag flag momentum, reversal trading, movie average trading, and opening range breakouts.

There are also advanced strategies that can be used to ensure the success of day trading. Three of these strategies are one stock in play, bull flag, and a fallen angel. With the use of these strategies, a successful trader builds his or her trading business step by step. The common steps involve building a watchlist, having a trading plan and knowing how to execute.

Made in the USA
Monee, IL
05 May 2023

2817c6d1-5352-4585-9e74-d4c0550807ecR01